The Essential K...

BETWEEN
NIGHT & MORN

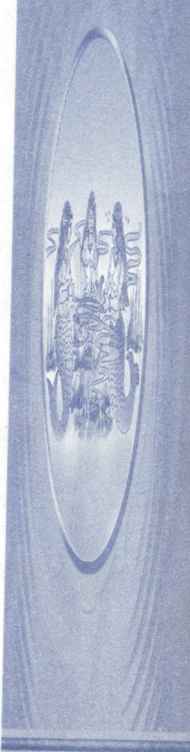

The Essential Kahlil Gibran

BETWEEN
NIGHT & MORN

KAHLIL GIBRAN

INDIANA
PUBLISHING HOUSE

2/13, Ansari Road, Darya Ganj
New Delhi-110 002

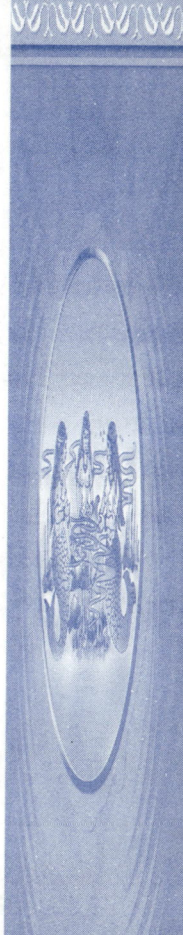

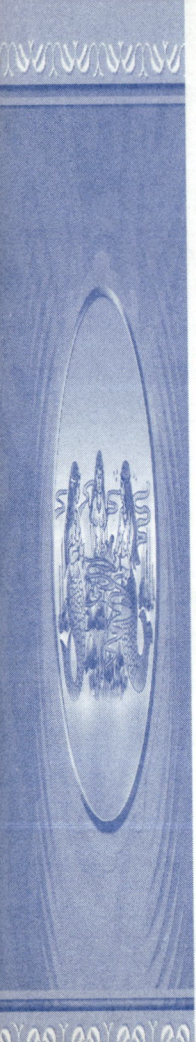

BETWEEN NIGHT & MORN
ISBN: 81-903188-6-1

First Edition : 2006

Published by :
INDIANA PUBLISHING HOUSE
2/13, Ansari Road, Darya Ganj
New Delhi - 110 002

Printed by :
Saurabh Printers Pvt. Ltd.
A-16, Sector-IV, NOIDA 201 301

PREFACE

Between Night and Morn enkindles an earthly hope and throws one into raptures of sheer exaltation for it assays to return all the blessings that God and Nature had restored upon mankind but this society chose to stagnate with its strict codes and conventions and divisions of humanity.

The book bestows knowledge of the sheer earthly elements, so imperative for existence. While on one hand, the author describes the exuberant beauty of his native country wherever he can, on the other he deals with inhuman bondages like slavery, conflict, warfare.

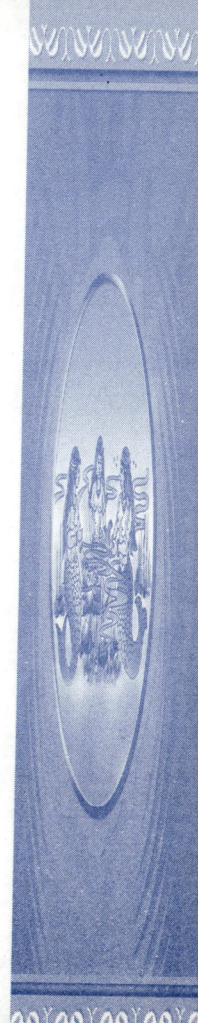

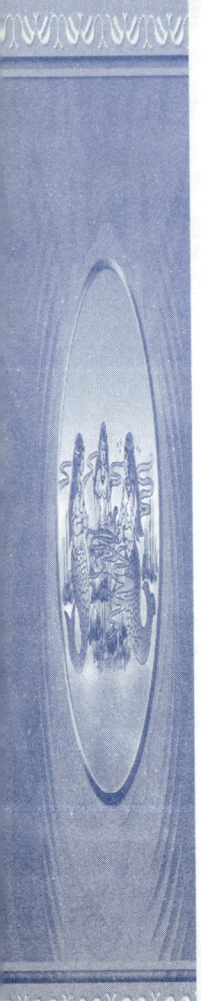

The book is concluded by a poem titled, Between Night and Morn.

Hence the darker side of society as well as the inherent positivity of people has held sway over the ingenius mental acumen of Kahlil Gibran. It is a book that will brighten your face with hope and vision, refresh the heart, lend a sparkle to your eyes and lend a smile to your lips—the gift from the Immortal Prophet of Lebanon.

"Rise, my heart, and raise your voice with music, for he who dares not Dawn with His songs is one of the sons of ever Darkness".

THE TEMPEST

PART ONE

YUSIF EL FAKHRI was thirty years of age when he withdrew himself from society and departed to live in an isolated hermitage in the vicinity of Kedeesha Valley in North Lebanon. The people of the nearby villages heard various tales concerning Yusif; some related that his was a wealthy and noble family, and that he loved a woman who betrayed him and caused him to lead a solitary life, while others said that he was a poet who deserted the clamourous city and retired to that place in order to record his thoughts and

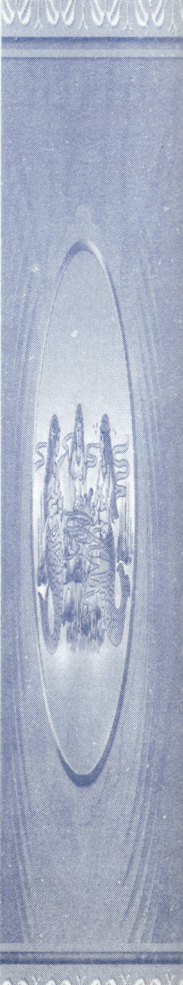

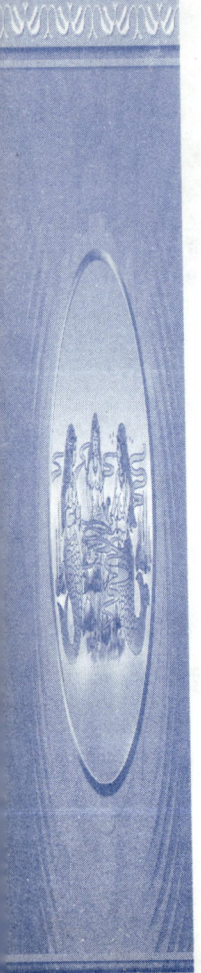

compose his inspiration; and many were sure that he was a mystic who was contented with the spiritual world, although most people insisted that he was a madman.

As for myself, I could not draw any conclusion regarding the man, for I knew that there must be a deep secret within his heart whose revelation I would not trust to mere speculation. I had long hoped for the opportunity to meet this strange man. I had endeavoured in devious ways to win his friendship in order to study his reality and learn his story by inquiring as to his purpose in life, but my efforts were in vain. When I met him for the first time, he was walking by the forest of the Holy Cedars of Lebanon, and I greeted him with the finest choice of words, but he returned my greeting by merely shaking his head and striding off.

On another occasion I found him standing in the midst of a small vineyard by a monastery, and again I approached and greeted him, saying, "It is said by the villagers that this monastery was built by a Syriac group in the Fourteenth Century; do you know anything of its history?" He replied coldly, "I do not know who built this monastery, nor do I care to know." And he turned his back to me and added, "Why do you not ask your grandparents, who are older than I, and who know more of the history of these valleys than I do?" Realizing at once my utter failure, I left him.

Thus did two years pass, and the bizarre

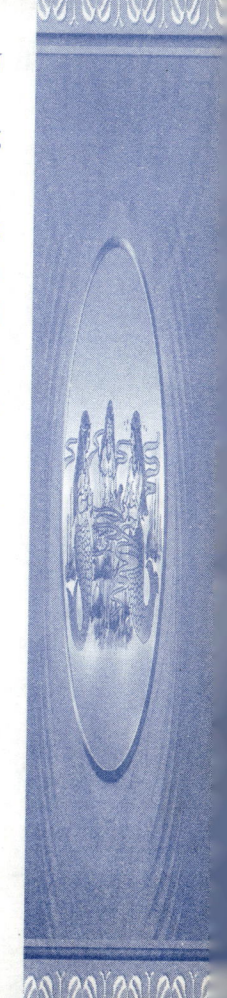

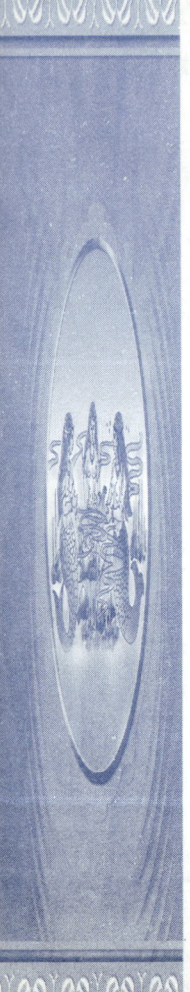

life of this strange man preyed on my mind
and disturbed my dreams.

PART TWO

One day in Autumn, as I was roaming the
hills and knolls adjacent to the hermitage of
Yusif El Fakhri, I was suddenly caught in a
strong wind and torrent rain, and the tempest
cast me here and there like a boat whose
rudder has been broken and whose masts have
been torn by a gale in a rough sea. I directed
my steps with difficulty toward Yusif's place,
saying to myself, "This is an opportunity I
have long sought, and the tempest will be my
excuse for entering, while my wet clothes will
serve as good reason for lingering."

I was in a miserable plight when I reached

the hermitage, and as I knocked on the door, the man whom I had been longing to see opened it. He was holding in one hand a dying bird whose head had been injured and whose wings had been broken. I greeted him saying, "I beg your forgiveness for this annoying intrusion. The raging tempest trapped me while I was afar from home." He frowned, saying, "There are many caves in this wilderness in which you might have taken refuge." However, he did not close the door, and the beat of my heart quickened in anticipation, for the realization of my great wish was close at hand. He commenced to touch the bird's head gently and with the utmost care and interest, exhibiting a quality important to my heart. I was surprised over

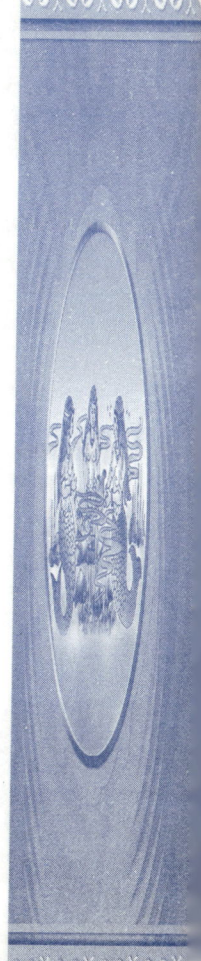

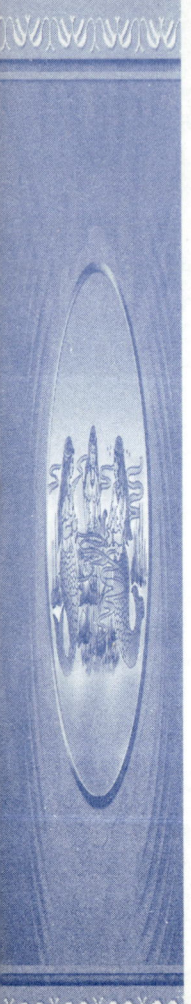

the two opponent characteristics I found in that man—mercy and cruelty at the same time. We became aware of the strained silence. He resented my presence, I desired to remain.

It seemed as if he felt my thought, for he looked up and said, "The tempest is clean, and declines to eat soured meat. Why do you seek to escape from it?" And with a touch of humour, I responded. "The tempest may not desire salted or soured things, but she is inclined to chill and tender all things, and undoubtedly she would enjoy consuming me if she grasped me again." His expression was severe when he retorted, "The tempest would have bestowed upon you a great honour, of which you are not worthy, if she had swallowed you." I agreed, "Yes, Sir, I fled the tempest so I might not be awarded an honour which I do not merit." He turned his face from me in an effort to choke his smile, and then motioned toward a wooden bench by the fireplace and invited me to rest and dry my raiment. I could scarcely control my elation.

I thanked him and sat down while he seated himself opposite, on a bench carved of rock. He commenced to dip his finger tips into an earthenware jar containing a kind of oil, applying it softly to the bird's head and wings. Without looking up he said, "The strong winds have caused this bird to fall upon the rocks between Life and Death.' I replied, rendering comparison, "And the strong winds have sent me, adrift, to your door, in time to

7

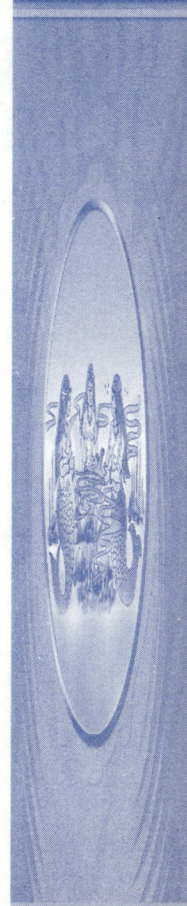

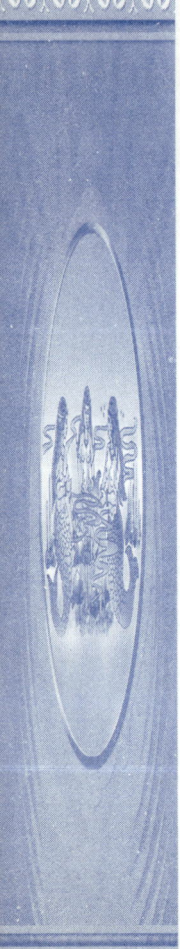

prevent having my head injured and my wings broken."

He looked at me seriously and said, "It is my wish that man would show the bird's instinct, and it is my wish that the tempest would break the people's wings. For man inclines toward fear and cowardice, and as he feels the awakening of the tempest he crawls into the crevices and the caves of the earth and hides himself."

My purpose was to extract the story of his self imposed exile, and I provoked, "Yes, the birds possess an honour and courage that man does not possess. . . . Man lives in the shadow of laws and customs which he made and fashioned for himself, but the birds live according to the same free Eternal Law which causes the earth to pursue its mighty path about the sun." His eyes and face brightened, as if he had found in me an understanding disciple, and he exclaimed, "Well done! If you place belief in your own words you should leave civilization and its corrupt laws and traditions, and live like the birds in a place empty of all things except the magnificent law of heaven and earth.

"Believing is a fine thing, but placing those beliefs into execution is a test of strength. Many are those who talk like the roar of the sea, but their lives are shallow and stagnant, like the rotting marshes. Many are those who lift their heads above the mountain tops, but their spirits remain dormant in the obscurity of the caverns." He rose trembling from his seat

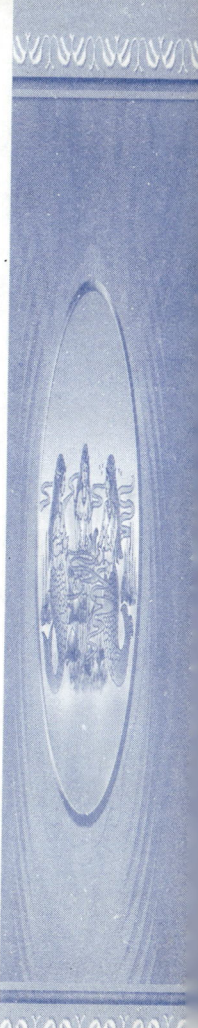

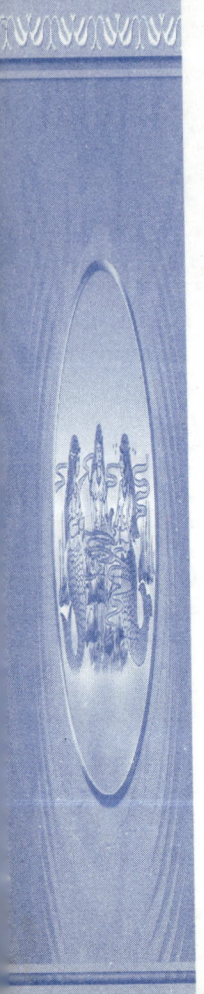

and placed the bird upon a folded cloth by the window.

He placed a bundle of dry sticks upon the fire, saying, "Remove your sandals and warm your feet, for dampness is dangerous to man's health. Dry well your garments, and be comfortable."

Yusif's continued hospitality kept my hopes high. I approached near to the fire, and the steam sifted from my wet robe. While he stood at the door gazing at the grey skies, my mind searched and scurried for the opening wedge into his background. I asked innocently, "Has it been long since you came to this place?

Without looking at me, he answered quietly, "I came to this place when the earth was without form, and void; and darkness was upon the face of the deep. And the Spirit of God moved upon the face of the waters."

I was aghast at these words! Struggling to gather my shocked and scattered wits, I said to myself, "How fantastic this man is! And how difficult is the path that leads to his reality! But I shall attack cautiously and slowly and patiently, until his reticence turns into communication, and his strangeness into understanding."

PART THREE

Night was spreading her black garment upon those valleys, and the tempest was shrieking dizzily and the rain becoming stronger. I began to fancy that the Biblical flood was coming again, to abolish life and

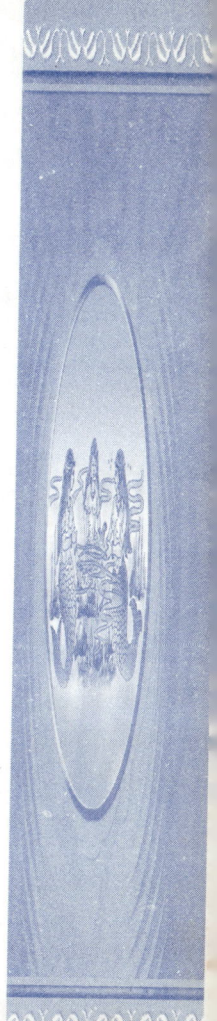

11

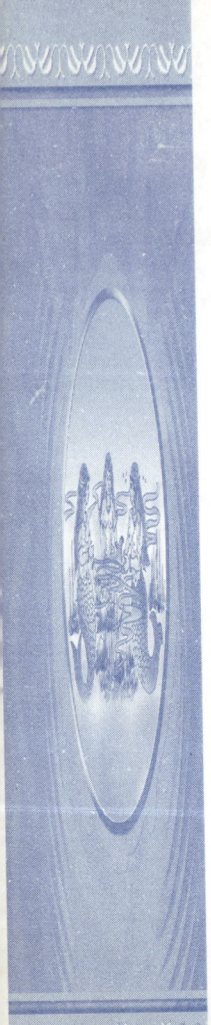

wash man's filth from God's earth.

It seemed that the revolution of elements had created in Yusif's heart a tranquility which often comes as a reaction to temperament and converts aloneness into conviviality. He ignited two candles, and then placed before me a jar of wine and a large tray containing bread, cheese, olives, honey, and some dry fruits. Then he sat near me, and after apologizing for the small quantity—but not for the simplicity—of the food, asked me to join him.

We partook of the repast in understanding silence, listening to the wailing of the wind and the crying of the rain, and at the same time I was contemplating his face and trying to dig out his secrets, meditating the possible motive underlying his unusual existence. Having finished, he took a copper kettle from the fire and poured pure, aromatic coffee into two cups; then he opened a small box and offered me a cigarette, addressing me as "Brother." I took one while drinking my coffee, not believing what my eyes were seeing. He looked at me smilingly, and after he had inhaled deeply of his cigarette and sipped some coffee, he said, "Undoubtedly you are thinking upon the existence here of wine and tobacco and coffee, and you may also be wondering over my food and comforts. Your curiosity is justified in all respects, for you are one of the many who believe that in being away from the people, one is absent from life, and must abstain from all its enjoyment." Quickly I agreed, "Yes, it is related by the wise men that he who deserts

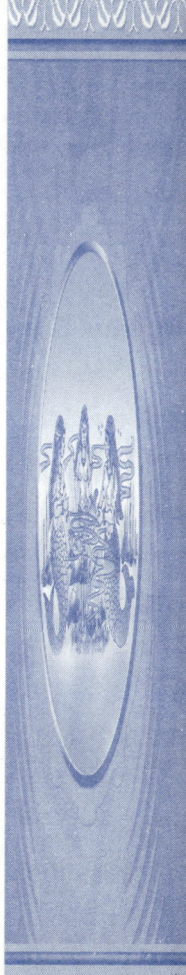

13

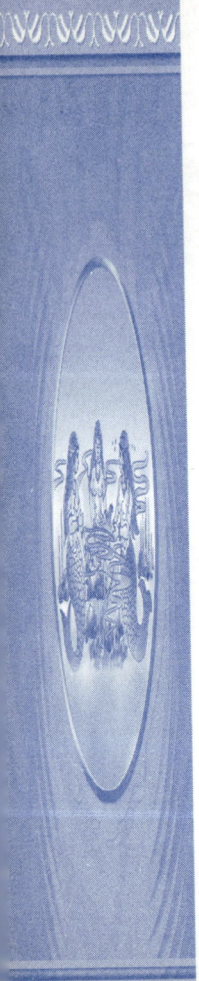

the world for the purpose of worshipping God alone will leave behind all the enjoyment and plenty of life, contenting himself with the simple products of God alone, and existing on plants and water."

After a pause, heavy with thought, he mused, "I could have worshipped God while living among His creatures, for worship does not require solitude. I did not leave the people in order to see God, for I had always seen Him at the home of my father and mother. I deserted the people because their natures were in conflict with mine, and their dreams did not agree with my dreams. . . . I left man because I found that the wheel of my soul was turning one way and grinding harshly against the wheels of other souls which were turning in the opposite direction. I left civilization because I found it to be an old and corrupt tree, strong and terrible, whose roots are locked into the obscurity of the earth and whose branches are reaching beyond the cloud; but its blossoms are of greed and evil and crime, and its fruit is of woe and misery and fear. Crusaders have undertaken to blend good into it and change its nature, but they could not succeed. They died disappointed, persecuted and torn."

Yusif leaned toward the side of the fireplace as if awaiting the impression of his words upon my heart. I thought it best to remain a listener, and he continued, "No, I did not seek solitude to pray and lead a hermit's life . . . for prayer, which is the song of the heart, will reach the ears of God even when mingled with the shout

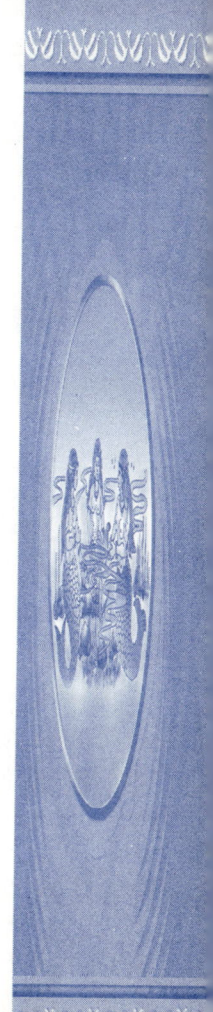

and cry of thousands of voices. To live the life of a recluse is to torture the body and soul and deaden the inclinations, a kind of existence which is repugnant to me, for God has erected the bodies as temples for the spirits, and it is our mission to deserve and maintain the trust reposed in us by God.

"No, my brother, I did not seek solitude for religious purposes, but solely to avoid the people and their laws, their teachings and their traditions, their ideas and their clamour and their wailing.

"I sought solitude in order to keep from seeing the faces of men who sell themselves and buy with the same price that which is lower than they are, spiritually and materially.

"I sought solitude in order that I might not encounter the women who walk proudly,

16

with one thousands smiles upon their lips, while in the depths of their thousands of hearts there is but one purpose.

"I sought solitude in order to conceal myself from those self-satisfied individuals who see the spectre of knowledge in their dreams and believe that they have attained their goal.

"I fled from society to avoid those who see but the phantom of truth in their awakening, and shout to the world that they have acquired completely the essence of truth.

"I deserted the world and sought solitude because I became tired of rendering courtesy to those multitudes who believe that humility is a sort of weakness, and mercy a kind of cowardice, and snobbery a form of strength.

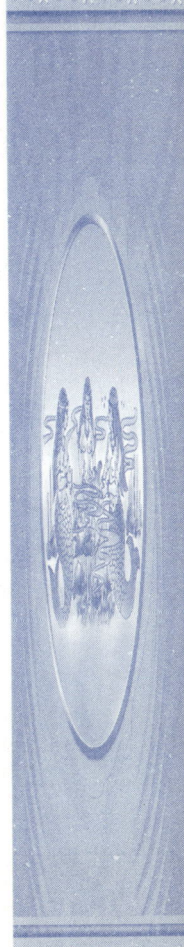

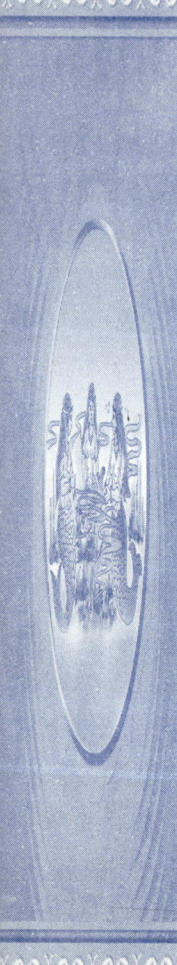

"I sought solitude because my soul wearied of association with those who believe sincerely that the sun and moon and stars do not rise save from their coffers, and do not set except in their gardens.

"I ran from the office-seekers who shatter the earthly fate of the people while throwing into their eyes the golden dust and filling their ears with sounds of meaningless talk.

"I departed from the ministers who do not live according to their sermons, and who demand of the people that which they do not solicit of themselves.

"I sought solitude because I never obtained kindness from a human unless I paid the full price with my heart.

"I sought solitude because I loathe that great and terrible institution which the people call civilization–that symmetrical monstrosity erected upon the perpetual misery of human kinds.

"I sought solitude for in it there is a full life for the spirit and for the heart and for the body. I found the endless prairies where the light of the sun rests, and where the flowers breathe their fragrance into space, and where the streams sing their way to the sea. I discovered the mountains where I found the fresh awakening of Spring, and the colourful longing of Summer, and the rich songs of Autumn, and the beautiful mystery of Winter. I came to this far corner of God's domain for I hungered to learn the secrets of the

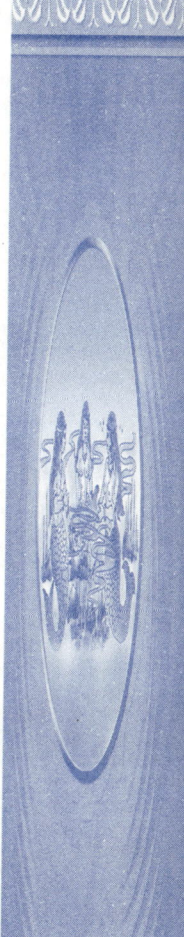

19

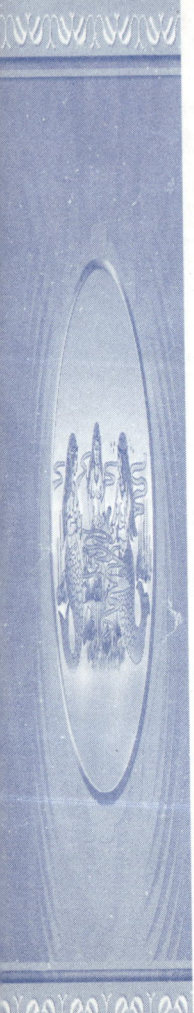

universe, and approach close to the throne of God."

Yusif breathed deeply, as if he had been relieved of a heavy burden. His eyes shone with strange and magical rays, and upon his radiant face appeared the signs of pride, will, and contentment.

A few minutes passed, and I was gazing placidly at him, and pondering the unveiling of what had been hidden from me; then I addressed him, saying, "You are undoubtedly correct in most of the things you have said, but through your diagnosis of the social ailment, you prove at the same time that you are a good doctor. I believe that the sick society is in dire need of such a physician, who should cure it or kill it. This distressed world begs your attention. Is it just or merciful to withdraw yourself from the ailing patient and deny him your benefit?"

He stared at me thoughtfully, and then said with futility, "Since the beginning of the world, the doctors have been trying to save the people from their disorders; some used knives, while others used potions, but pestilence spread hopelessly. It is my wish that the patient would content himself with remaining in his filthy bed, meditating his long-continued sores; but instead, he stretches his hands from under the robe and clutches at the neck of each who comes to visit him, choking him to death. What irony it is! The evil patient kills the doctor, and then closes his eyes and says within himself, 'He was a

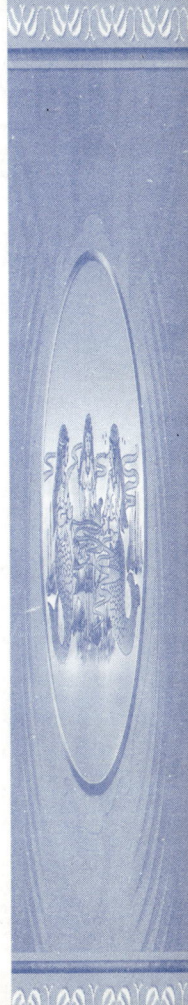

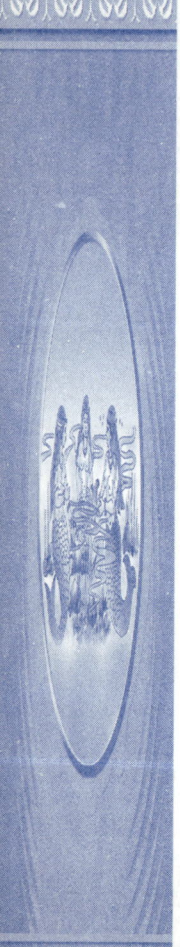

great physician.' No, Brother, no one on earth can benefit humanity. The sower, however wise and expert he may be, cannot cause the field to sprout in Winter."

And I argued, "The people's Winter will pass away, and then comes the beautiful Spring, and the flower must surely bloom in the fields, and the brooks will again leap in the valleys."

He frowned, and said bitterly, "Alas! Has God divided man's life—which is the whole creation—into seasons like those of the year? Will any tribe of human beings, living now in God's truth and spirit, desire to re-appear on the face of this earth? Will ever the time come when man settles and abides at the right arm of Life, rejoicing with the brilliant light of day and the peaceful silence of night? Can that dream become reality? Can it materialize after the earth has been covered with human flesh and drenched with man's blood?"

And Yusif stood and raised his hand toward the sky, as if pointing at a different world, and he continued, "This is naught but a vain dream for the world, but I am finding its accomplishment for myself, and what I am discovering here occupies every space in my heart and in the valleys and in the mountains." He now raised his intense voice, "What I really know to be true is the crying of my inner self. I am here living, and in the depths of my existence there is a thirst and hunger, and I find joy in partaking of the bread and wine of Life from the vases which

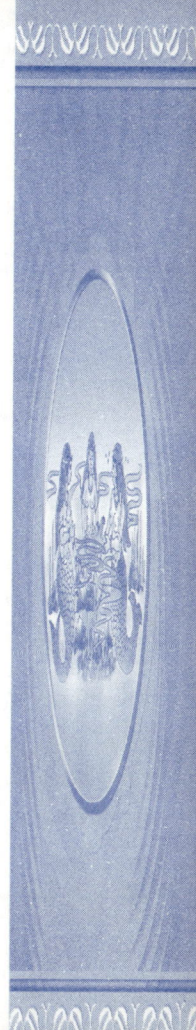

23

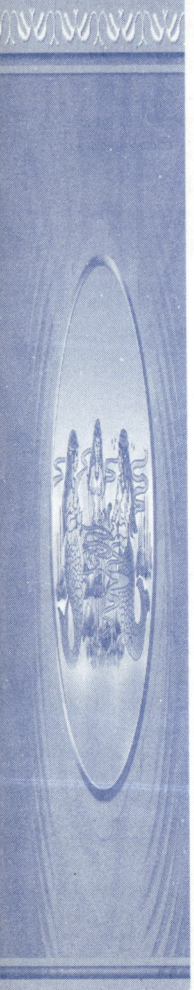

I make and fashion by my own hands. For this reason I abandoned the boards of the people and came to this place, and I shall remain here until the Ending!"

He continued walking back and forth across the room in agitation while I was pondering his sayings and meditating the description of society's gaping wounds. I ventured again a tactful criticism. "I hold the utmost regard for your opinion and intentions, and I envy and respect your solitude and aloneness, but I know that this miserable nation has sustained a great loss in your expatriation, for she is in need of an understanding healer to help her through her difficulties and awaken her spirit."

He shook his head slowly and said, "This

nation is like all the nations. And the people are made of the same element and do not vary except in their exterior appearance, which is of no consequence. The misery of our Oriental nations is the misery of the world, and what you call civilization in the West is naught but another spectre of the many phantoms of tragic deception.

"Hypocrisy will always remain, even if her finger tips are coloured and polished; and Deceit will never change even if her touch becomes soft and delicate; and Falsehood will never turn into Truth even if you dress her with silken robes and place her in the palace; and Greed will not become Contentment; nor will Crime become Virtue. And Eternal Slavery to teachings, to customs, and to history will

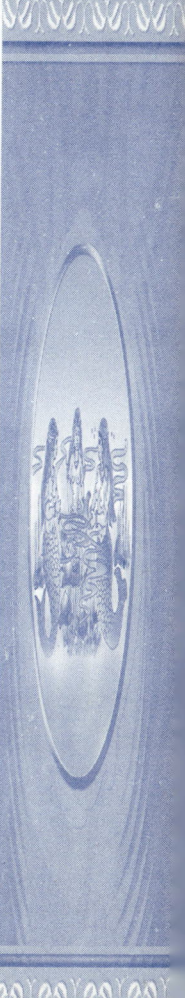

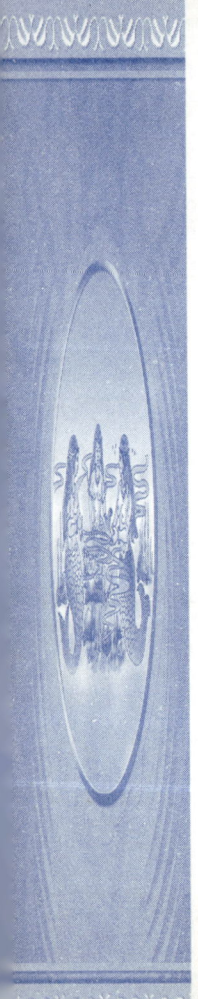

remain Slavery even if she paints her face and disguises her voice. Slavery will remain Slavery in all her horrible form, even if she calls herself Liberty.

"No, my brother, the West is not higher than the East, nor is the West lower than the East, and the difference that stands between the two is not greater than the difference between the tiger and the lion. There is a just and perfect law that I have found behind the exterior of society, which equalizes misery, prosperity, and ignorance; it does not prefer one nation to another, nor does it oppress one tribe in order to enrich another."

I exclaimed, "Then civilization is vanity, and all in it is vanity!" He quickly responded, "Yes, civilization is vanity and all in it is vanity. . . . Inventions and discoveries are but amusement and comfort for the body when it is tired and weary. The conquest of distance and the victory over the seas are but false fruit which do not satisfy the soul, nor nourish the heart, neither lift the spirit, for they are afar from nature. And those structures and theories which man calls knowledge and art are naught except shackles and golden chains which man drags, and he rejoices with their glittering reflections and ringing sounds. They are strong cages whose bars man commenced fabricating ages ago, unaware that he was building from the inside, and that he would soon become his own prisoner to eternity. Yes, vain are the deeds of man, and vain are his purposes, and all is

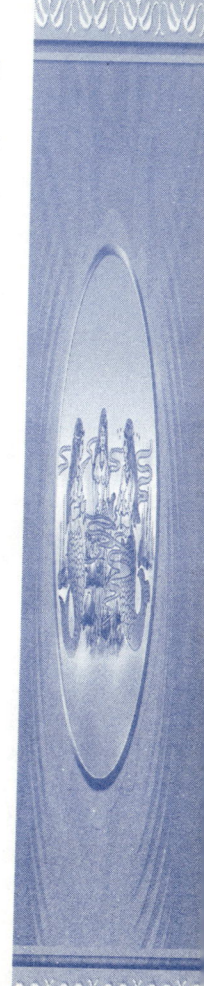

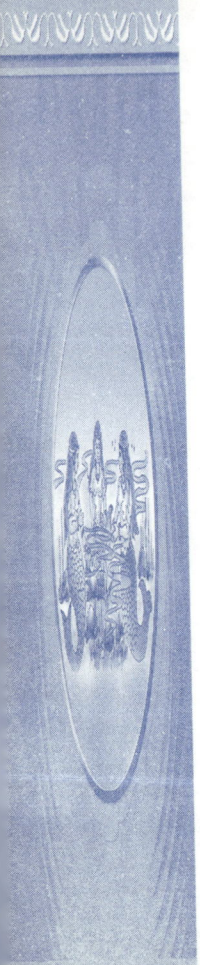

vanity upon the earth." He paused, then slowly added, "And among all vanities of life, there is only one thing that the spirit loves and craves. One thing dazzling and alone."

"What is it?" I inquired with quivering voice. He looked at me for a long minute and then closed his eyes. He placed his hands on his chest, while his face brightened, and with a serene and sincere voice he said, "It is an awakening in the spirit; it is an awakening in the inner depths of the heart; it is an overwhelming and magnificent power that descends suddenly upon man's conscience and opens his eyes, whereupon he sees Life amid a dizzying shower of brilliant music, surrounded by a circle of great light, with man standing as a pillar of beauty between the earth and the firmament. It is a flame that suddenly rages

28

within the spirit and sears and purifies the heart, ascending above the earth and hovering in the spacious sky. It is a kindness that envelops the individual's heart whereby he would bewilder and disapprove all who opposed it, and revolt against those who refuse to understand its great meaning. It is a secret hand which removed the veil from my eyes while I was a member of society amidst my family, my friends and my countrymen.

"Many times I wondered, and spoke to myself saying, "What is this Universe, and why am I different from those people who are looking at me, and how do I know them, and where did I meet them, and why am I living among them? Am I a stranger among them, or is it they who are strange to this earth, built by Life who entrusted me with the keys?"

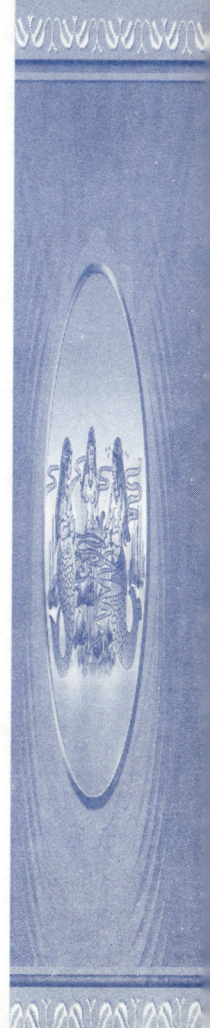

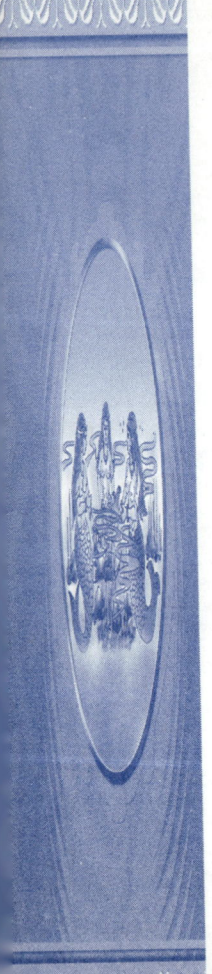

He suddenly became silent, as if remembering something he had seen long before, refusing to reveal it. Then he stretched his arms forward and whispered, "That is what happened to me four years ago, when I left the world and came to this void place to live in the awakeness of life and enjoy kind thoughts and beautiful silence."

He walked toward the door, looking at the depths of the darkness as if preparing to address the tempest. But he spoke in a vibrating voice, saying, "It is an awakening within the spirit; he who knows it, is unable to reveal it by words; and he who knows it not, will never think upon the compelling and beautiful mystery of existence."

PART FOUR

An hour had passed and Yusif El Fakhri was striding about the room, stopping at random and gazing at the tremendous grey skies. I remained silent, reflecting upon the strange unison of joy and sorrow in his solitary life.

Later in the night he approached me and stared long into my face, as if wanting to commit to memory the picture of the man to whom he had disclosed the piercing secrets of his life. My mind was heavy with turmoil, my eyes with mist. He said quietly, "I am going now to walk through the night with the tempest, to feel the closeness of Nature's expression; it is a practise that I enjoy greatly in Autumn and Winter. Here is the wine, and

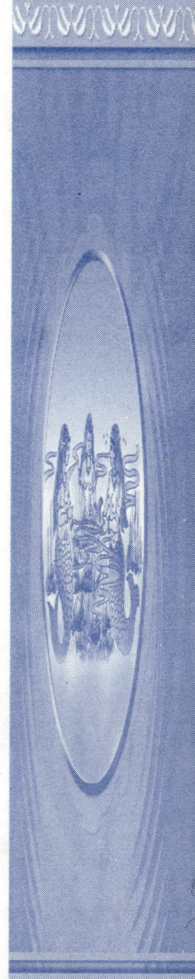

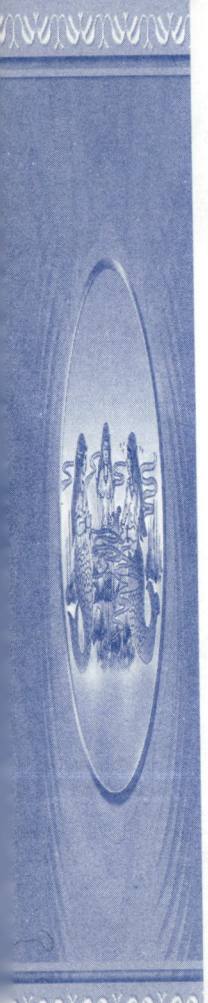

there is the tobacco; please accept my home as your own for the night."

He wrapped himself in a black robe and added smilingly, "I beg you to fasten the door against the intruding humans when you leave in the morning, for I plan to spend the day in the forest of the Holy Cedars." Then he walked toward the door, carrying a long walking staff and he concluded, "If the tempest surprises you again while you are in this vicinity, do not hesitate to take refuge in this hermitage....I hope you will teach yourself to love, and not to fear, the tempest...Good night, my brother."

He opened the door and walked out with his head high, into the dark. I stood at the door to see which course he had taken, but he had disappeared from view. For a few minutes I heard the fall of his feet upon the broken stones of the valley.

PART FIVE

Morning came, after a night of deep thought, and the tempest had passed away, while the sky was clear and the mountains and the plains were reveling in the sun's warm rays. On my way back to the city I felt that spiritual awakening of which Yusif El Fakhri had spoken, and it was raging throughout every fibre of my being. I felt that my shivering must be visible. And when I calmed, all about me was beauty and perfection.

As soon as I reached the noisome people and heard their voices and saw their deeds, I

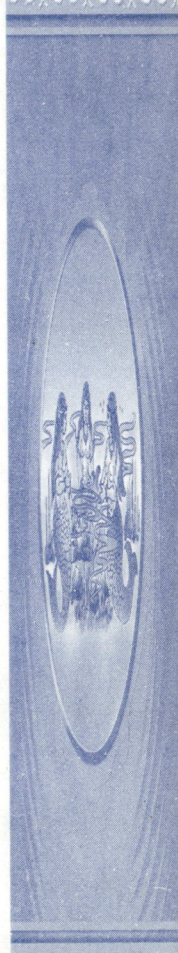

stopped and said within myself, "Yes, the spiritual awakening is the most essential thing in man's life, and it is the sole purpose of being. Is not civilization, in all its tragic forms, a supreme motive for spiritual awakening? Then how can we deny existing matter, while its very existence is unwavering proof of its conformability into the intended fitness? The present civilization may possess a vanishing purpose, but the eternal law has offered to that purpose a ladder whose steps can lead to a free substance."

I never saw Yusif El Fakhri again, for through my endeavours to attend the ills of civilization, Life and expelled me from North Lebanon in late Autumn of that same year, and I was required to live in exile in a distant country whose tempests are domestic. And leading a hermit's life in that country is a sort of glorious madness, for its society, too, is ailing.

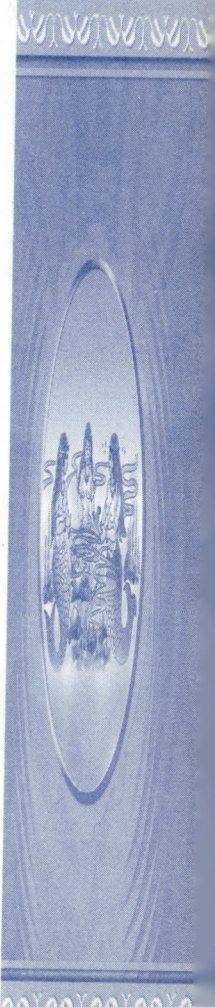

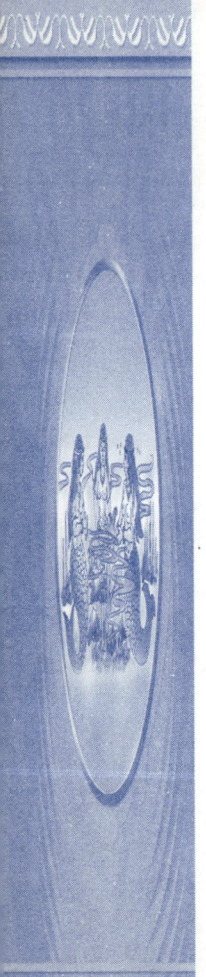

SLAVERY

THE people are the slaves of Life, and it is slavery which fills their days with misery and distress, and floods their nights with tears and anguish.

Seven thousand years have passed since the day of my first birth, and since that day I have been witnessing the slaves of Life, dragging their heavy shackles.

I have roamed the East and West of the earth and wandered in the Light and in the Shadow of Life. I have seen the processions of civilization moving from light into darkness, and each was dragged down to hell by humiliated souls bent under the yoke of slavery. The strong is fettered and subdued, and the faithful is on his knees worshipping before the idols. I have followed man from Babylon to Cairo, and from Ain Dour to Baghdad, and observed the marks of his chains upon the sand. I heard the sad echoes of the fickle ages repeated by the eternal prairies and valleys.

I visited the temples and altars and entered the palaces, and sat before the thrones. And I saw the apprentice slaving for the artisan, and the artisan slaving for the employer, and the employer slaving for the soldier, and the soldier slaving for the governor, and the governor slaving for the king, and the king slaving for the priest, and the priest slaving

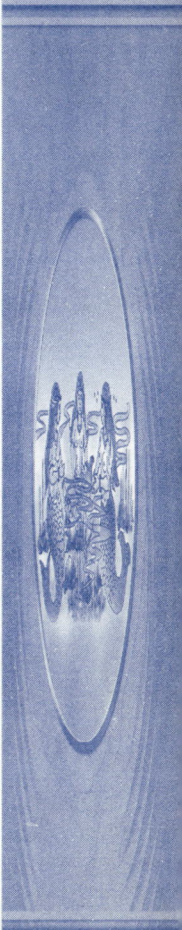

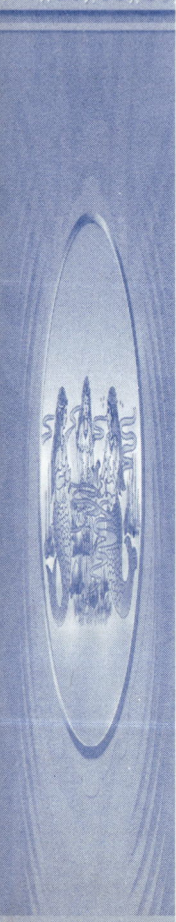

for the idol…..And the idol is naught but earth fashioned by Satan and erected upon a knoll of skulls.

I entered the mansions of the rich and visited the huts of the poor. I found the infant nursing the milk of slavery from his mother's bosom, and the children learning submission with the alphabet.

The maidens wear garments of restriction and passivity, and the wives retire with tears upon beds of obedience and legal compliance.

I accompanied the ages from the banks of the Kange to the shores of Euphrates; from the mouth of the Nile to the plains of Assyria; from the arenas of Athens to the churches of Rome; from the slums of Constantinople to the palaces of Alexandria…… Yet I saw slavery moving over all, in a glorious and majestic procession of ignorance. I saw the people sacrificing the youths and maidens at the feet of the idol, calling her the God; pouring wine and perfume upon her feet, and calling her the Queen; burning incense before her image, and calling her the Prophet; kneeling and worshipping before her, and calling her the Law; fighting and dying for her, and calling her Patriotism; submitting to her will, and calling her the Shadow of God on earth; destroying and demolishing homes and institutions for her sake, and calling her Fraternity; struggling and stealing and working for her, and calling her Fortune and Happiness; killing for her, and calling her Equality.

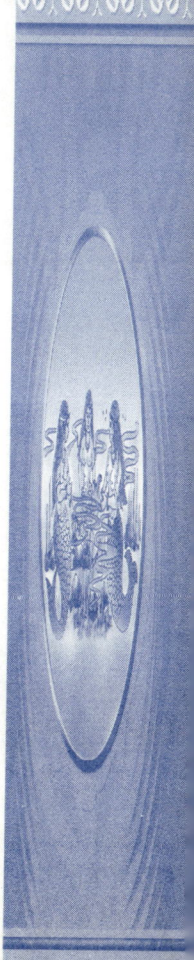

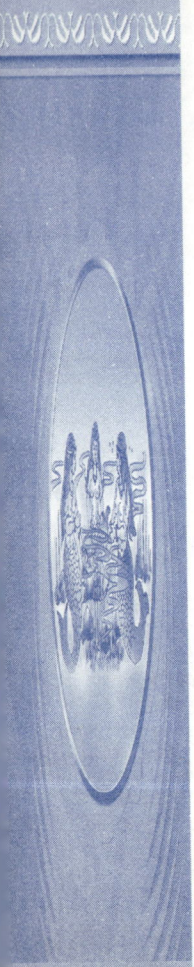

She possesses various names, but one reality. She has many appearances, but is made of one element. In truth, she is an everlasting ailment bequeathed by each generation unto its successor.

I found the blind slavery, which ties the people's present with their parents' past, and urges them to yield to their traditions and customs, placing ancient spirits in the new bodies.

I found the mute slavery, which binds the life of a man to a wife whom he abhors, and places the woman's body in the bed of a hated husband, deadening both lives spiritually.

I found the deaf slavery, which stifles the soul and the heart, rendering man but an empty echo of a voice, and a pitiful shadow of a body.

I found the lame slavery, which places man's neck under the domination of the tyrant and submits strong bodies and weak minds to the sons of Greed for use as instruments to their power.

I found the ugly slavery, which descends with the infants' spirits from the spacious firmament into the home of Misery, where Need lives by Ignorance, and Humiliation resides beside Despair. And the children grow as miserables, and live as criminals, and die as despised and rejected non-existents.

I found the subtle slavery, which entitles things with other than their names-calling slyness an intelligence, and emptiness a knowledge, and weakness a tenderness, and cowardice a strong refusal.

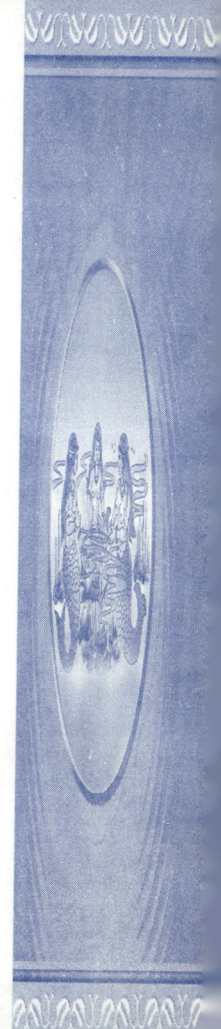

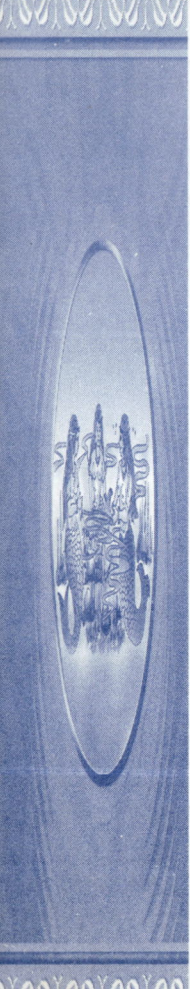

I found the twisted slavery, which causes the tongues of the weak to move with fear, and speak outside of their feelings, and they feign to be meditating their plight, but they become as empty sacks, which even a child can fold or hang.

I found the bent slavery, which prevails upon one nation to comply with the laws and rules of another nation, and the bending is greater with each day.

I found the perpetual slavery, which crowns the sons of monarchs as kings, and offers no regard to merit.

I found the black slavery, which brands with shame and disgrace forever the innocent sons of the criminals.

Contemplating slavery, it is found to

possess the vicious powers of continuation and contagion.

When I grew tired of following the dissolute ages, and wearied of beholding the processions of stoned people, I walked lonely in the Valley of the Shadow of Life, where the past attempts to conceal itself in guilt, and the soul of the future folds and rests itself too long. There, at the edge of Blood and Tears River, which crawled like a poisonous viper and twisted like a criminal's dreams, I listened to the frightened whisper of the ghosts of slaves, and gazed at nothingness.

When midnight came and the spirits emerged from hidden places, I saw a cadaverous, dying spectre fall to her knees, gazing at the moon. I approached her, asking,

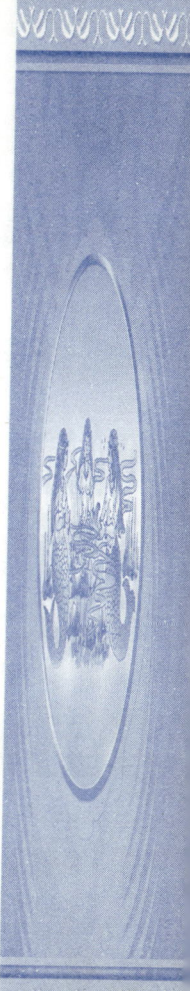

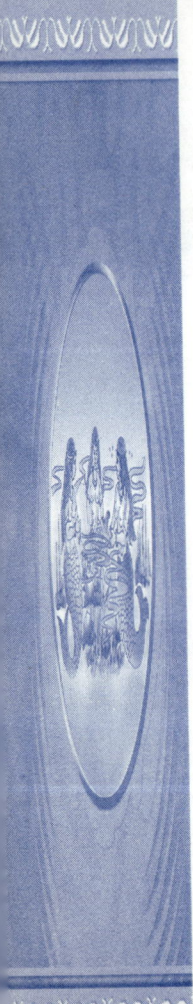

"What is your name?"

"My Name is Liberty," replied this ghastly shadow of a corpse.

And I inquired. "Where are your children?"

And Liberty, tearful and weak, gasped, "One died crucified another died mad, and third one is not yet born."

She limped away and spoke further, but the mist in my eyes and cries of my heart prevented sight or hearing.

SATAN

THE people looked upon Father Samaan as their guide in the field of spiritual and theological matters, for he was an authority and a source of deep information on venial and mortal sins, well versed in the secrets of Paradise, Hell, and Purgatory.

Father Samaan's mission in North Lebanon was to travel from one village to another, preaching and curing the people from the spiritual disease of sin, and saving them from the horrible trap of Satan. The Reverend Father waged constant war with Satan. The fellahin honoured and respected this clergyman, and were always anxious to buy his advice or

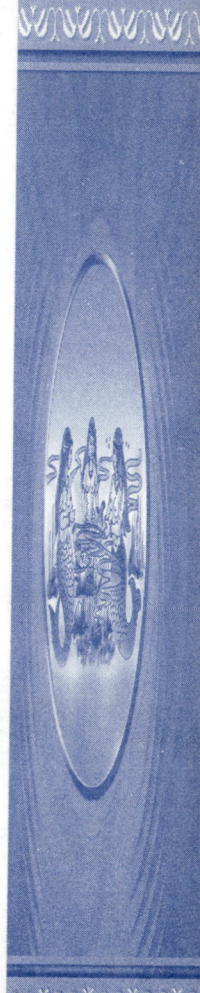

45

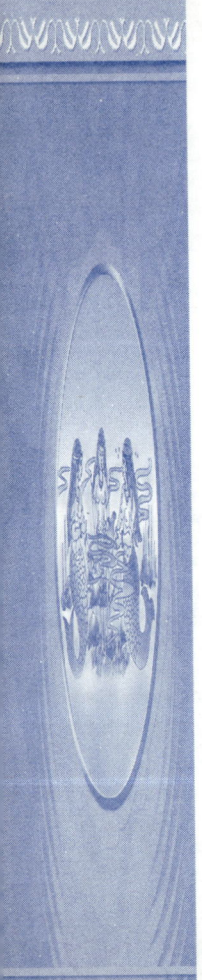

prayers with pieces of gold and silver; and at every harvest they would present him with the finest fruits of their fields.

One evening in Autumn, as Father Samaan walked his way toward a solitary village, crossing those valleys and hills, he heard a painful cry emerging from a ditch at the side of the road. He stopped and looked in the direction of the voice, and saw an unclothed man lying on the ground. Streams of blood oozed from deep wounds in his head and chest. He was moaning pitifully for aid, saying, "Save me, help me. Have mercy on me, I am dying." Father Samaan looked with perplexity at the sufferer, and said within himself, "This man must be a thief....He probably tried to rob the wayfarers and failed. Some one has wounded him, and I fear that should he die I may be accused of having taken his life."

Having thus pondered the situation, he resumed his journey, whereupon the dying man stopped him, calling out, "Do not leave me! I am dying!" Then the Father meditated again, and his face became pale as he realized he was refusing to help. His lips quivered, but he spoke to himself, saying, "He must surely be one of the madmen wandering in the wilderness. The sight of his wounds brings fear into my heart; what shall I do? Surely a spiritual doctor is not capable of treating flesh-wounded bodies." Father Samaan walked ahead a few paces when the near-corpse uttered a painful plaint that melted the heart of the rock and he gasped, "Come close to me! Come, for we have been

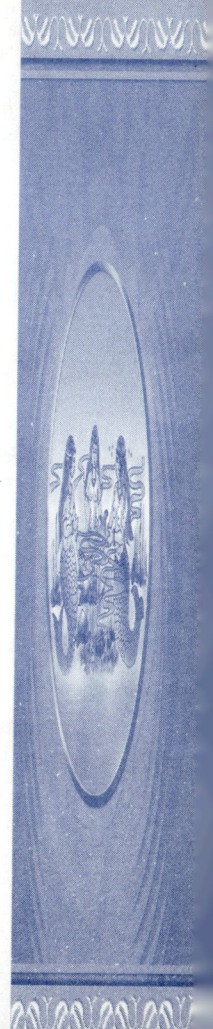

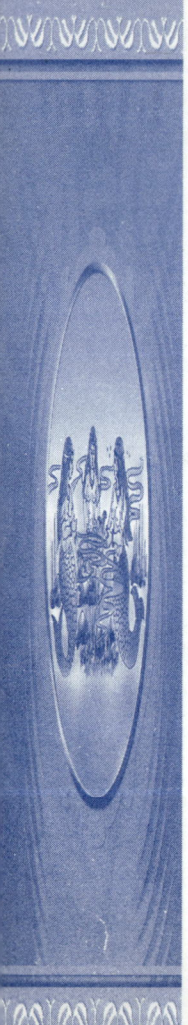

friends a long time….. You are Father Samaan, the Good Shepherd, and I am not a thief nor a madman….Come close, and do not let me die in this deserted place. Come, and I will tell you who I am."

Father Samaan came close to the man, knelt, and stared at him; but he saw a strange face with contrasting features; he saw intelligence with slyness, ugliness with beauty, and wikedness with softness. He withdrew to his feet sharply, and exclaimed, "Who are you?"

With a fainting voice, the dying man said, "Fear me not, Father, for we have been strong friends for long. Help me to stand, and take me to the nearby streamlet and cleanse my wounds with your linens." And the Father inquired, "Tell me who you are, for I do not know you, nor even remember having seen you."

And the man replied with an agonizing voice, "You know my identity! You have seen me one thousand times and you speak of me each day....I am dearer to you than your own life." And the Father reprimanded, "You are a lying imposter! A dying man should tell the truth....I have never seen your evil face in my entire life. Tell me who you are, or I will suffer you to die, soaked in your own escaping life." And the wounded man moved slowly and looked into the clergyman's eyes, and upon his lips appeared a mystic smile; and in a quiet, deep and smooth voice he said, "I am Satan."

Upon hearing the fearful word, Father

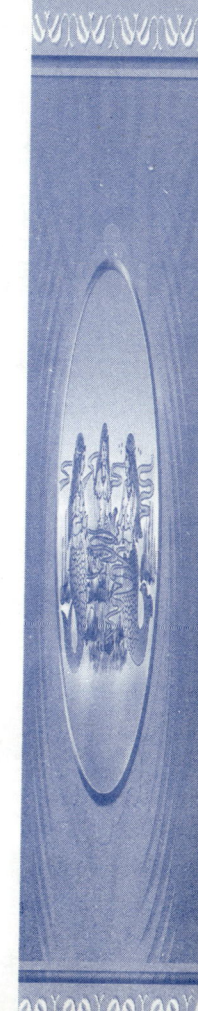

49

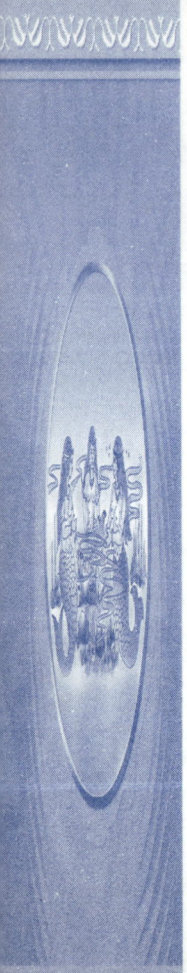

Samaan uttered a terrible cry that shook the far corners of the valley; then he stared, and realized that the dying man's body with its grotesque distortions, coincided with the likeness of Satan in a religious picture hanging on the wall of the village church. He trembled and cried out, saying, "God has shown me your hellish image and justly caused me to hate you; cursed be you forevermore! The mangled lamb must be destroyed by the shepherd lest he will infect the other lambs!"

Satan answered, "Be not in haste, Father, and lose not this fleeting time in empty talk.....Come and close my wounds quickly, before Life departs from my body." And the clergyman retorted, "The hands which offer a daily sacrifice to God shall not touch a body

50

made of the secretion of Hell.....You must die accursed by the tongues of the Ages, and the lips of Humanity, for you are the enemy of Humanity, and it is your avowed purpose to destroy all virtue."

Satan moved in anguish, raising himself upon one elbow, and responded, "You know not what you are saying, nor understand the crime you are committing upon yourself. Give heed, for I will relate my story. Today I walked alone in this solitary valley. When I reached this place, a group of angels descended to attack, and struck me severely; had it not been for one of them, who carried a blazing sword with two sharp edges, I would have driven them off, but I had no power against the brilliant sword." And Satan ceased

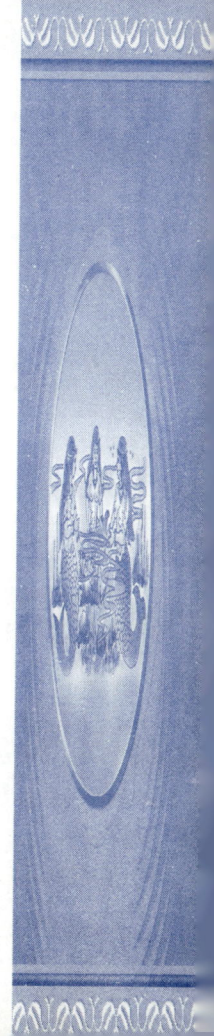

51

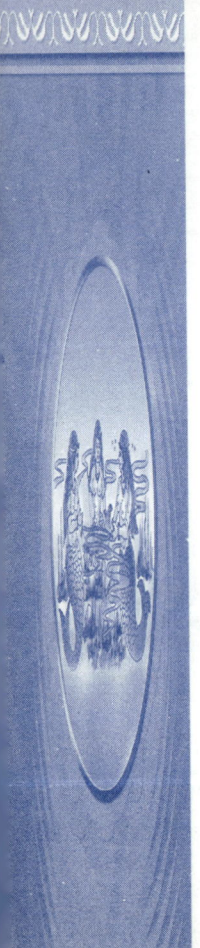

talking for a moment, as he pressed a shaking hand upon a deep wound in his side. Then he continued, "The armed angel—I believe he was Michael—was an expert gladiator. Had I not thrown myself to the friendly ground and feigned to have been slain, he would have torn me into brutal death."

With voice of triumph, and casting his eyes heavenward, the Father offered, "Blessed be Michael's name, who has saved Humanity from this vicious enemy."

And Satan protested, "My disdain for Humanity is not greater than your hatred for yourself...... You are blessing Michael who never has come to your rescue.....You are cursing me in the hour of my defeat, even though I was, and still am, the source of your tranquility and happiness....you deny me your blessing, and extend not your kindness, but you live and prosper in the shadow of my being.... You have adopted for my existence an excuse and weapon for your career, and you employ my name in justification for your deeds. Has not my past caused you to be in need of my present and future! Have you reached your goal in amassing the required wealth? Have you found it impossible to extract more gold and silver from your followers, using my kingdom as a threat?

"Do you not realize that you will starve to death if I were to die? What would you do tomorrow if you allowed me to die today? What vocation would you pursue if my name disappeared? For decades you have been roaming these villages and warning the people

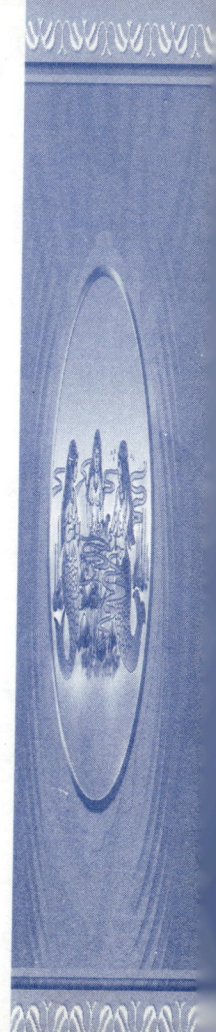

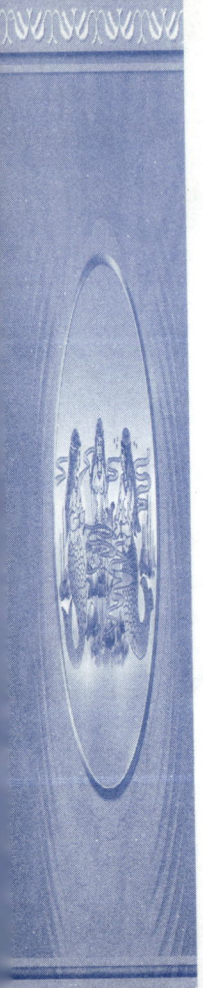

against falling into my hands. They have bought your advice with their poor denars and with the products of their land. What would they buy from you tomorrow, if they discovered that their wicked enemy no longer existed? Your occupation would die with me, for the people would be safe from sin. As a clergyman, do you not realize that Satan's existence alone has created his enemy, the church? That ancient conflict is the secret hand which removes the gold and silver from the faithful's pocket and deposits it forever into the pouch of the preacher and missionary. How can you permit me to die here, when you know it will surely cause you to lose your prestige, your church, your home, and your livelihood?"

Satan became silent for a moment and his humility was now converted into a confident independence, and he continued, "Father, you are proud, but ignorant. I will disclose to you the history of belief, and in it you will find the truth which joins both of our beings, and ties my existence with your very conscience.

"In the first hour of the beginning of time, man stood before the face of the sun and stretched forth his arms and cried for the first time, saying, "Behind the sky there is a great and loving and benevolent God." Then man turned his back to the great circle of light and saw his shadow upon the earth, and he hailed, 'In the depths of the earth there is a dark devil who loves wickedness.'

"And the man walked toward his cave,

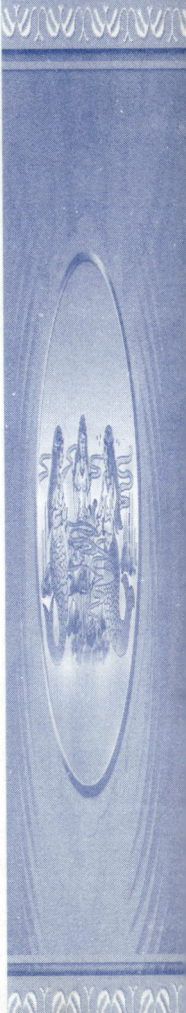

whispering to himself, 'I am between two compelling forces, one in whom I must take refuge, and the other against whom I must struggle.' And the ages marched in procession while man existed between two powers, one that he blessed because it exalted him, and one that he cursed because it frightened him. But he never perceived the meaning of a blessing or of a curse; he was between the two, like a tree between Summer, when it blooms, and Winter, when if shivers.

"When man saw the dawn of civilization, which is human understanding, the family as a unit came into being. Then came the tribes, whereupon labour was divided according to ability and inclination; one clan cultivated the land, another built shelters, others wove raiment or hunted food. Subsequently divination made its appearance upon the earth, and this was the first career adopted by man which possessed no essential urge or necessity."

Satan ceased talking for a moment. Then he laughed and his mirth shook the empty valley, but his laughter reminded him of his wounds, and he placed his hand on his side, suffering with pain. He steadied himself and continued, "Divination appeared and grew on earth in strange fashion.

"There was a man in the first tribe called La Wiss. I know not the origin of his name. He was an intelligent creature, but extremely indolent and he detested work in the cultivation of land, construction of shelters, grazing of cattle or any pursuit requiring body

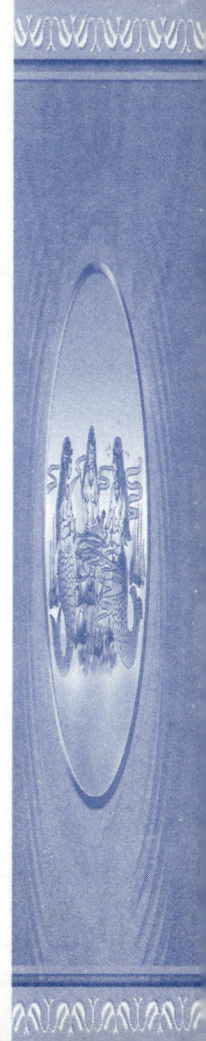

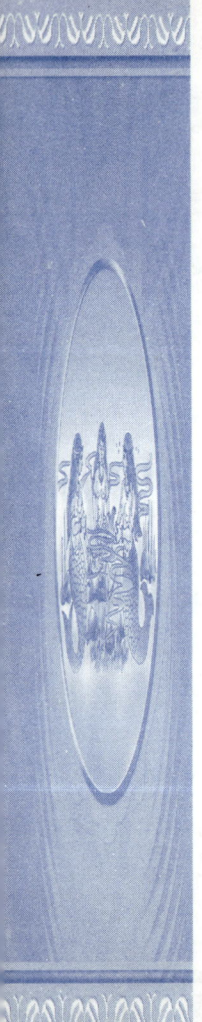

movement or exertion. And since food, during that era, could not be obtained except by arduous toil, La Wiss slept many nights with an empty stomach.

"One Summer night, as the members of that clan were gathered around the hut of their Chief, talking of the outcome of their day and waiting for their slumber time, a man suddenly leaped to his feet, pointed toward the moon, and cried out, saying, 'Look at the Night God! His face is dark, and his beauty has vanished, and he has turned into a black stone hanging in the dome of the sky!' The multitude gazed at the moon, shouted in awe, and shook with fear, as if the hands of darkness had clutched their hearts, for they saw the Night God slowly turning into a dark ball which changed the bright countenance of the earth and caused the hills and valleys before their eyes to disappear behind a black veil.

"At that moment, La Wiss, who had seen an eclipse before, and understood its simple cause, stepped forward to make much of this opportunity. He stood in the midst of the throng, lifted his hands to the sky, and in a strong voice he addressed them, saying, 'Kneel and pray, for the Evil God of Obscurity is locked in struggle with the Illuminating Night God; if the Evil God conquers him, we will all perish, but if the Night God triumphs over him, we will remain alive...Pray now and worship... Cover your faces with earth....close your eyes, and lift not your heads toward the sky, for he who witnesses the two gods wrestling will lose

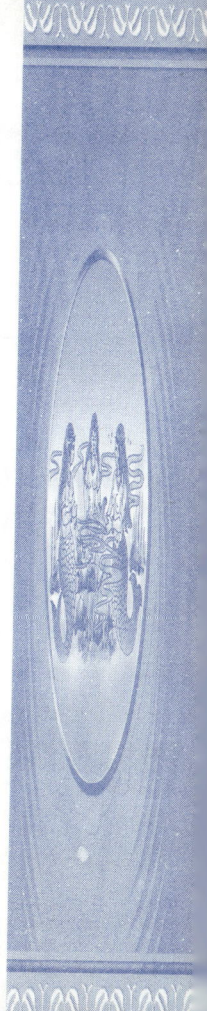

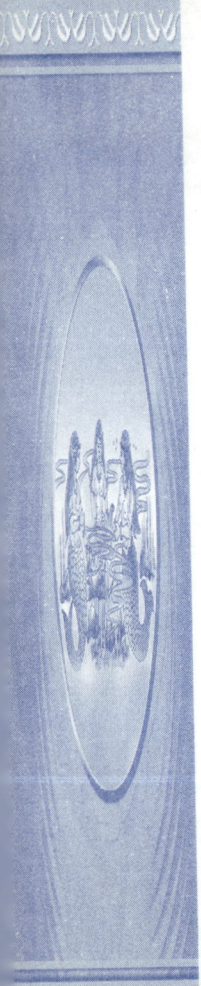

his sight and mind, and will remain blind and insane all his life! Bend your heads low, and with all your hearts urge the Night God against his enemy, who is our mortal enemy!'

"Thus did La Wiss continue talking, using many cryptic words of his own fabrication which they had never heard. After this crafty deception, as the moon returned to its previous glory, La Wiss raised his voice louder than before and said impressively, "Rise now, and look at the Night God who has triumphed over his evil enemy. He is resuming his journey among the stars. Let it be known that through your prayers you have helped him to overcome the Devil of Darkness. He is well pleased now, and brighter than ever."

The multitude rose and gazed at the moon that was shining in full beam. Their fear became tranquility, and their confusion was now joy. They commenced dancing and singing and striking with their thick sticks upon sheets of iron, filling the valleys with their clamour and shouting

"That night, the Chief of the tribe called La Wiss and spoke to him, saying, 'You have done something that no man has ever done.....You have demonstrated knowledge of a hidden secret that no other among us understands. Reflecting the will of my people you are to be the highest ranking member, after me, in the tribe. I am the strongest man, and you are the wisest and most learned person....You are the medium between our

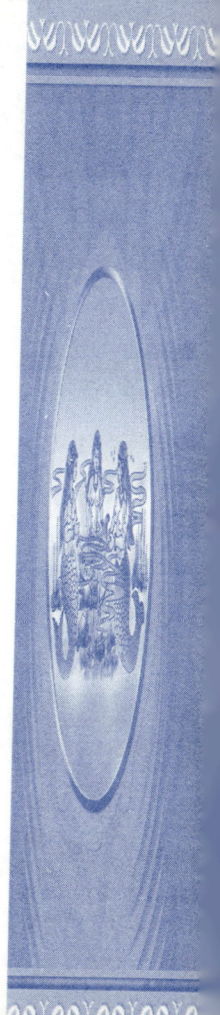

61

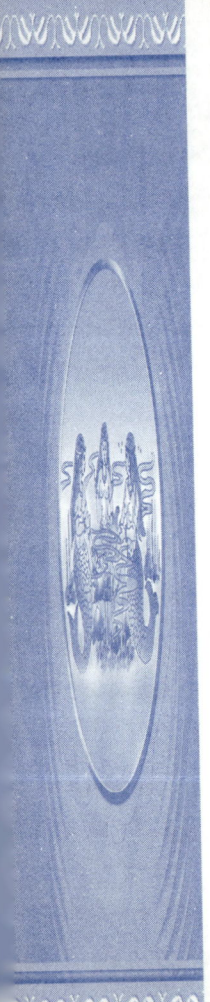

people and the gods, whose desires and deeds you are to interpret, and you will teach us those things necessary to gain their blessings and love.'

"And La Wiss slyly assured. 'Everything the Human God reveals to me in my divine dreams will be conveyed to you in awakeness, and you may be confident that I will act directly between you and him.' The chief was assured, and gave La Wiss two horses, seven calves, seventy sheep and seventy lambs; and he spoke to him, saying, 'The men of the tribe shall build for you a strong house, and we will give you at the end of each harvest season a part of the crop of the land so you may live as an honourable and respected Master.'

"La Wiss rose and started to leave, but the

Chief stopped him, saying, 'Who and what is
the one whom you call the Human God? Who
is this daring God who wrestles with the
glorious Night God? We have never pondered
him before,' La Wiss rubbed his forehead and
answered him, saying, 'My Honourable Master,
in the olden time, before the creation of man,
all the Gods were living peacefully together in
an upper world behind the vastness of the
stars. The God of Gods was their father, and
knew what they did not know, and did what
they were unable to do. He kept for himself
the divine secrets that existed beyond the eternal
laws. During the seventh epoch of the twelfth
age, the spirit of Bahtaar, who hated the great
God, revolted and stood before his father, and
said, 'Why do you keep for yourself the power

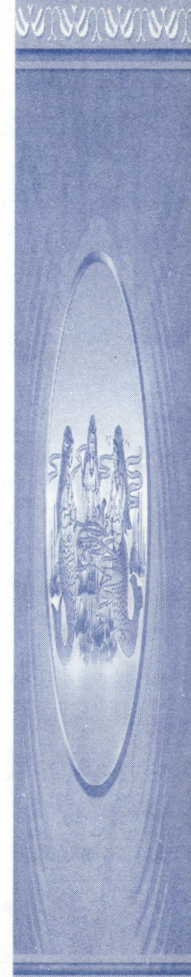

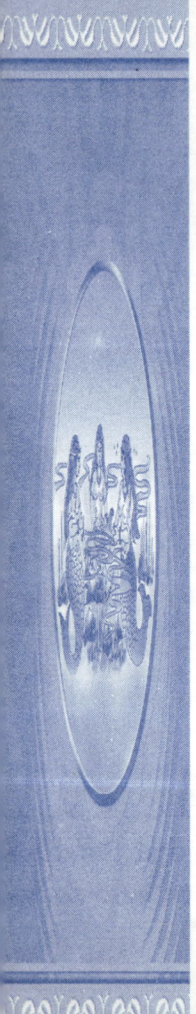

of great authority upon all creatures, hiding away from us the secrets and laws of the Universe? Are we not your children who believe in you and share with you the great understanding and the perpetual being?'

"The God of Gods became enraged and said, 'I shall preserve for myself the primary power and the great authority and the essential secrets, for I am the beginning and the end.'

"And Bahtaar answered him saying, 'Unless you share with me your might and power, I and my children and my children's children will revolt against you!' At that moment, the God of Gods stood upon his throne in the deep heavens, and drew forth a sword, and grasped the Sun as a shield; and with a voice that shook all corners of eternity he shouted out, saying, 'Descend, you evil rebel, to the dismal

64

lower world where darkness and misery exist! There you shall remain in exile, wandering until the Sun turns into ashes and the stars into dispersed particles!' In that hour, Bahtaar descended from the upper world into the lower world, where all the evil spirits dwelt. Thereupon, he swore by the secret of Life that he would fight his father and brothers by trapping every soul who loved them.'

"As the Chief listened, his forehead wrinkled and his face turned pale. He ventured, 'Then the name of the Evil God is Bahtaar?' and La Wiss responded, 'His name was Bahtaar when he was in upper world, but when he entered into the lower world, he adopted successively the names Baalzaboul, Satanail, Balial, Zamiel, Ahriman, Mara, Abdon, Devil and finally Satan, which is the

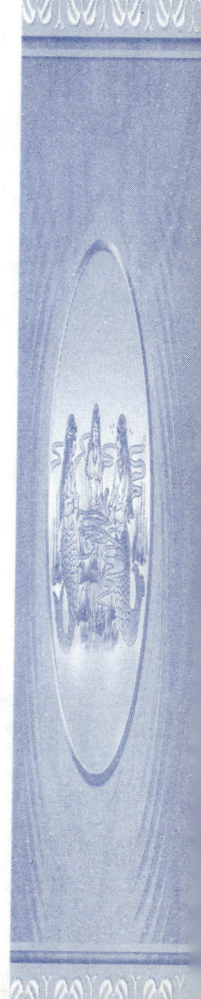

65

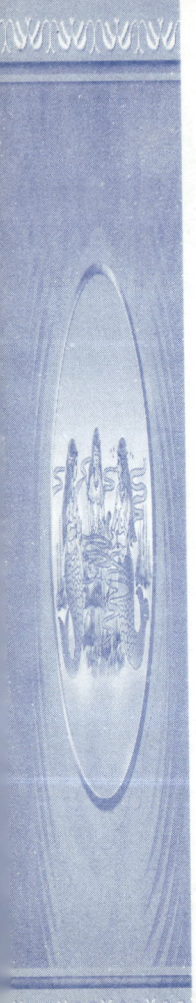

most famous.'

"The Chief repeated the word 'Satan' many times with a quivering voice that sounded like the rustling of the dry branches as the passing of the wind; then he asked, 'Why does Satan hate man as much as he hates the gods?' "

"And La Wiss responded quickly, 'He hates man because man is a descendant of Satan's brothers and sisters'. The Chief exclaimed, 'Then Satan is the cousin of man!' In a voice mingled with confusion and annoyance, he retorted, 'Yes, Master, but he is their great enemy who fills their days with misery and their nights with horrible dreams. He is the power who directs the tempest toward their hovels, and brings famine upon their plantation, and disease upon them and their animals. He is an evil and powerful god; he is wicked, and he rejoices when we are in sorrow, and he mourns when we are joyous. We must, through my knowledge, examine him thoroughly, in order to avoid his evil; we must study his character, so we will not step upon his trap-laden path.'

"The Chief leaned his head upon his thick stick and whispered, saying, 'I have learned now the inner secret of that strange power who directs the tempest toward our homes and brings the pestilence upon us and our cattle. The people shall learn all that I have comprehended now, and La Wiss will be blessed, honoured and glorified for revealing to them the mystery of their powerful enemy, and directing them away from the road of evil.'

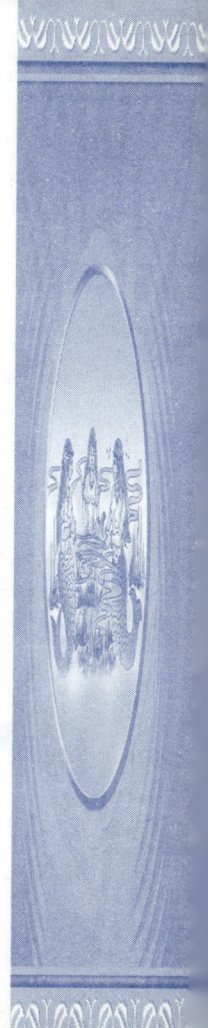

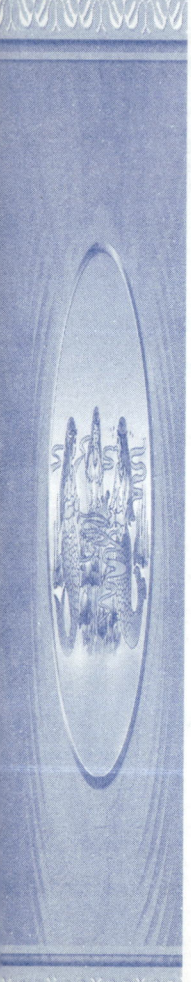

"And La Wiss left the Chief of the tribe and went to his retiring place, happy over his ingenuity, and intoxicated with the wine of his pleasure and fancy. For the first time, the Chief and all the tribe, except La Wiss, spent the night slumbering in beds surrounded by horrible ghosts, fearful spectres, and disturbing dreams."

Satan ceased talking for a moment, while Father Samaan stared at him as one bewildered, and upon the Father's lips appeared the sickly laughter of Death. Then Satan continued, "Thus divination came to this earth, and thus was my existence the cause for its appearance. La Wiss was the first who adopted my cruelty as a vocation. After the death of La Wiss, this occupation circulated through his children and prospered until it became a perfect and divine profession, pursued by those whose minds are ripe with knowledge, and whose souls are noble, and whose hearts are pure, and whose fancy is vast.

"In Babylon, the people bowed seven times in worshipping before a priest who fought me with his chantings.....In Nineveh, they looked upon a man, who claimed to have known my inner secrets, as a golden link between God and man.....In Tibet, they called the person who wrestled with me. The Son of the Sun and Moon.....In Byblus, Ephesus and Antioch, they offered their children's lives in sacrifice to my opponents....In Jerusalem and Rome, they placed their lives in the hands of those who claimed they hated me and fought me with all

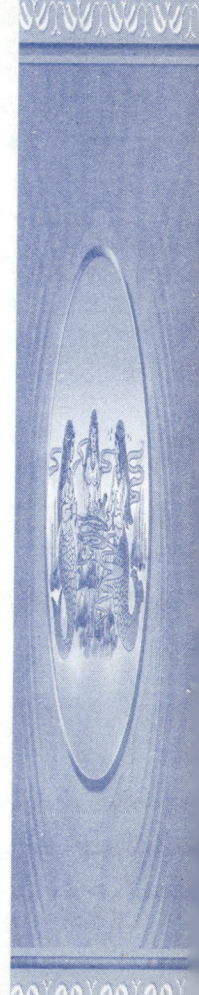

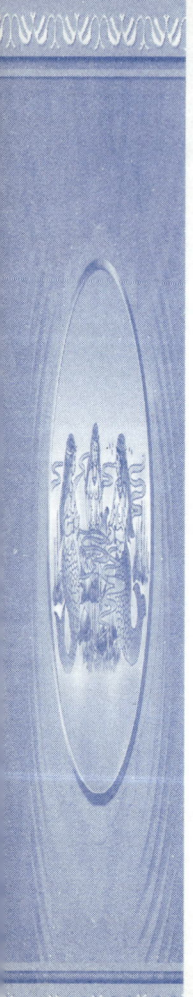

their might.

"In every city under the sun my name was the axis of the education circle of religion, arts and philosophy. Had it not been for me, no temples would have been built, no towers or palaces would have been erected. I am the courage that creates resolution in man....I am the source that provokes originality of thought....I am the hand that moves man's hands....I am Satan everlasting. I am Satan whom the people fight in order to keep themselves alive. If they cease struggling against me, slothfulness will deaden their minds and hearts and souls, in accordance with the weird penalties of their tremendous myth.

"I am the enraged and mute tempest who agitates the minds of man and the hearts of women. And in fear of me, they will travel to places of worship to condemn me, or to places of vice to make me happy by surrendering to my will. The monk who prays in the silence of the night to keep me away from his bed is like the prostitute who invites me to her chamber. I am Satan everlasting and eternal.

"I am the builder of convents and monasteries upon the foundation of fear. I build wine shops and wicked houses upon the foundations of lust and self-gratification. If I cease to exist, fear and enjoyment will be abolished from the world, and through their disappearance, desires and hopes will cease to exist in the human heart. Life will become empty and cold, like a harp with broken strings. I am Satan everlasting.

"I am the inspiration for Falsehood, Slander, Treachery, Deceit and Mockery, and

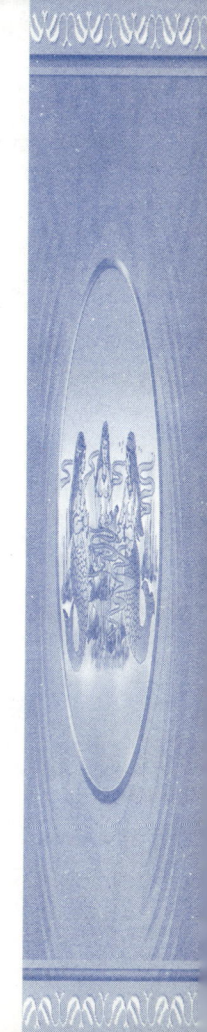

71

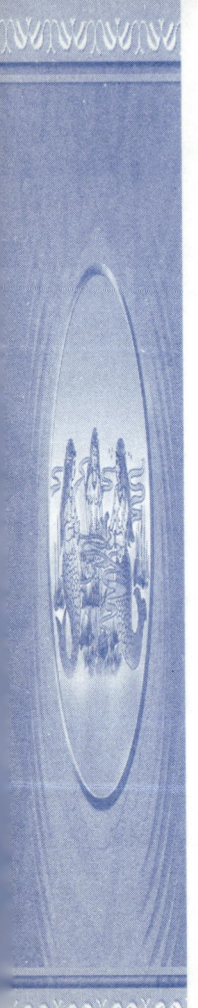

if these elements were to be removed from this world, human society would become like a deserted field in which naught would thrive but thorns of virtue. I am Satan everlasting.

"I am the father and mother of sin, and if sin were to vanish, the fighters of sin would vanish with it, along with their families and structures.

"I am the heart of all evil. Would you wish for human motion to stop through cessation of my heart beats? Would you accept the result after destroying the cause? I am the cause! Would you allow me to die in this deserted wilderness? Do you desire to sever the bond that exists between you and me! Answer me, clergyman!"

And Satan stretched his arms and bent his

head forward and gasped deeply; his face
turned to grey and he resembled one of those
Egyptian statues laid waste by the Ages at
the side of the Nile. Then he fixed his
glittering eyes upon Father Samaan's face, and
said, in a faltering voice. "I am tired and
weak. I did wrong by using my waning
strength to speak on things you already knew.
Now you may do as you please....You may
carry me to your home and treat my wounds,
or leave me in this place to die."

Father Samaan quivered and rubbed his
hands nervously, and with apology in his voice
he said, "I know now what I had not know
an hour ago. Forgive my ignorance. I know
that your existence in this world creates
temptation, and temptation is a measurement
by which God adjudges the value of human

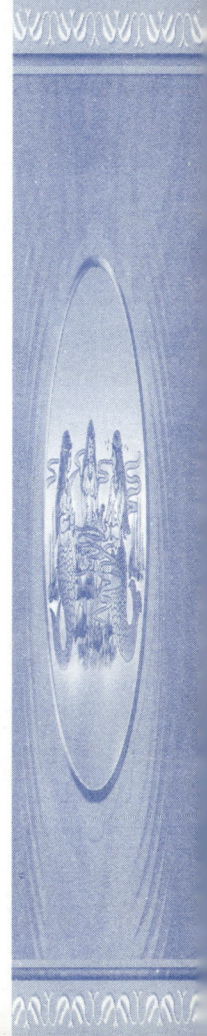

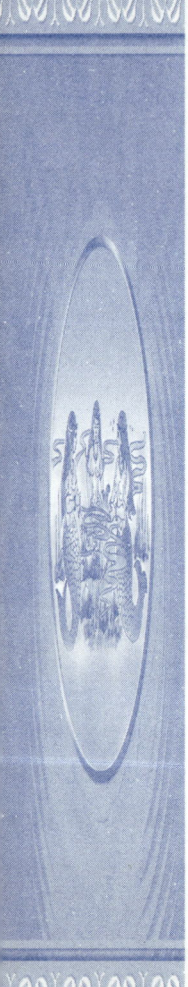

souls. It is a scale which Almighty God uses to weigh the spirits. I am certain that if you die, temptation will die, and with its passing, death will destroy the ideal power which elevates and alerts man.

"You must live, for if you die and the people know it, their fear of hell will vanish and they will cease worshipping, for naught would be sin. You must live, for in your life is the salvation of humanity from vice and sin.

"As to myself, I shall sacrifice my hatred for you on the altar of my love for man."

Satan uttered a laugh that rocked the ground, and he said, "What an intelligent person you are, Father! And what wonderful knowledge you possess in theological facts!

You have found, through the power of your knowledge, a purpose for my existence which I had never understood, and now we realize our need for each other.

"Come close to me, my brother; darkness is submerging the plains, and half of my blood has escaped upon the sand of this valley, and naught remains of me but the remnants of a broken body which Death shall soon buy unless you render aid." Father Samaan rolled the sleeves of his robe and approached, and lifted Satan to his back and walked toward his home.

In the midst of those valleys, engulfed with silence and embellished with the veil of darkness, Father Samaan walked toward the village with his back bent under his heavy

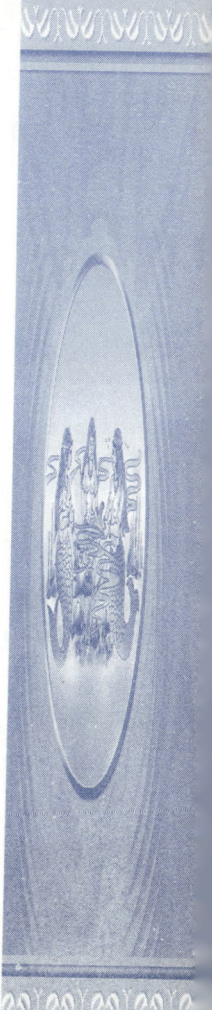

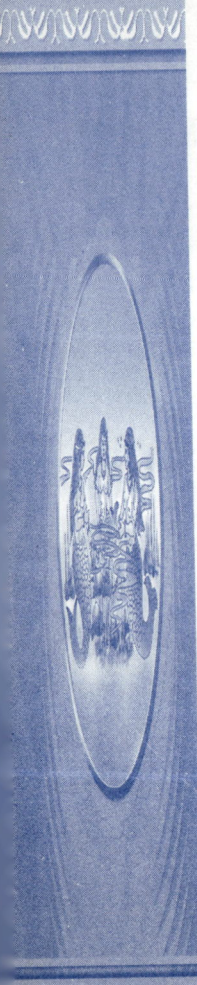

burden. His black raiment and long beard were spattered with blood streaming from above him, but he struggled forward, his lips moving in fervent prayer for the life of the dying Satan.

THE MERMAIDS

IN the depths of the sea, surrounding the nearby islands where the sun rises, there is a profoundness. And there, where the pearl exists in abundance, lay a corpse of a youth encircled by sea maidens of long golden hair, they stared upon him with their deep blue eyes, conversing among themselves with musical voices. And the conversation, heard by the depths and conveyed to the shore by the waves, was brought to me by the frolicsome breeze.

One of them said, "This is a human who entered into our world yesterday, while our sea was raging."

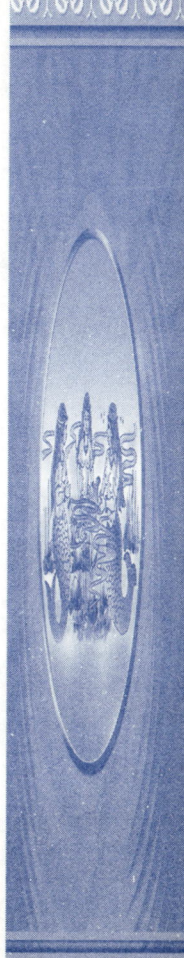

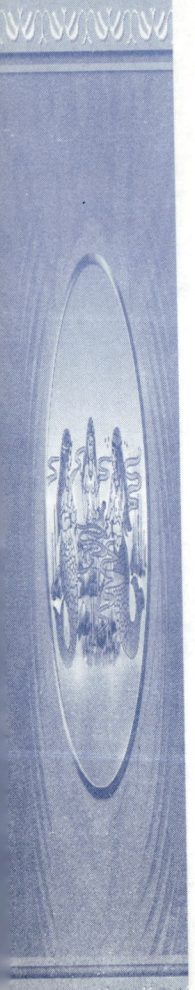

And the second one said, "The sea was not raging. Man, who claims that he is a descendant of the Gods, was making iron war, and his blood is being shed until the colour of the water is now crimson; this human is a victim of war."

The third one ventured, "I do not know what war is, but I do know that man, after having subdued the land, became aggressive and resolved to subdue the sea. He devised a strange object which carried him upon the seas, whereupon our severe Neptune became enraged over his greed. In order to please Neptune, man commenced offering gifts and sacrifices, and the still body before us is the most recent gift of man to our great and terrible Neptune."

The fourth one asserted, "How great is Neptune, and how cruel is his heart! If I were the Sultan of the sea I would refuse to accept such payment......Come now, and let us examine this ransom. Perhaps we may enlighten ourselves as to the human clan."

The mermaids approached the youth, probed the pockets, and found a message close to his heart; one of them read it aloud to the others:

"My Beloved:

"Midnight has again come, and I have no consolation except my pouring tears, and naught to comfort me save my hope in your return to me from between the bloody paws of war. I cannot forget your words when you took departure: 'Every man has a trust of tears

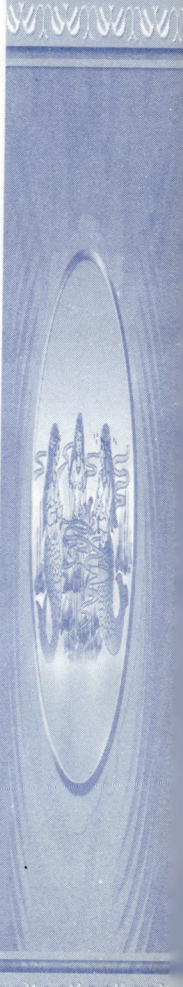

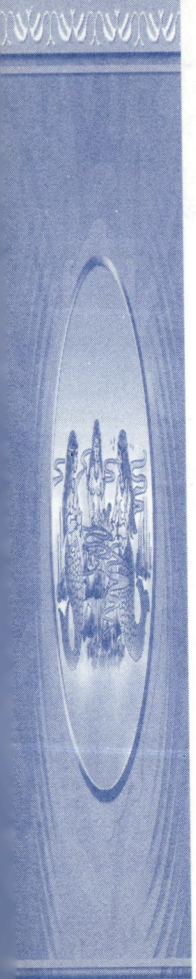

which must be returned some day.'

"I know not what to say, My Beloved, but my soul will pour itself into parchment.....my soul that suffers through separation, but is consoled by Love that renders pain a joy, and sorrow a happiness. When Love unified our hearts, and we looked to the day when our two hearts would be joined by the mighty breath of God, War shouted her horrible call and you followed her, prompted by your duty to the leaders.

"What is this duty that separates the lovers, and causes the women to become widows, and the children to become orphans? What is this patriotism which provokes wars and destroys kingdoms through trifles? And what cause can be more than trifling when compared to but one life? What is this duty which invites poor villagers, who are looked upon as nothing by the strong and by the sons of the inherited nobility, to die for the glory of their oppressors? If duty destroys peace among nations, and patriotism disturbs the tranquility of man's life, then let us say, 'Peace be with duty and patriotism.'

"No, no, My Beloved! Heed not my words! Be courageous and faithful to your country.....Hearken not unto the talk of a damsel, blinded by Love, and lost through farewell and aloneness....If Love will not restore you to me in this life, then Love will surely join us in the coming life.

Your Forever"

The mermaids replaced the note under the

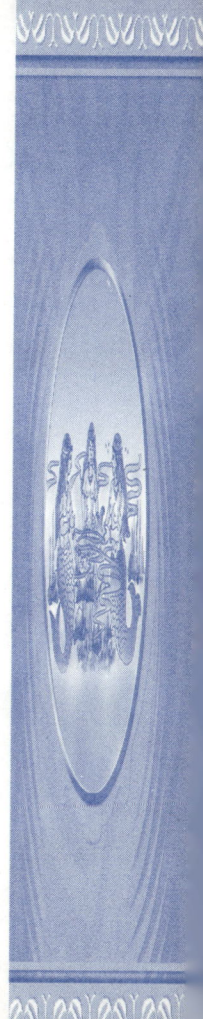

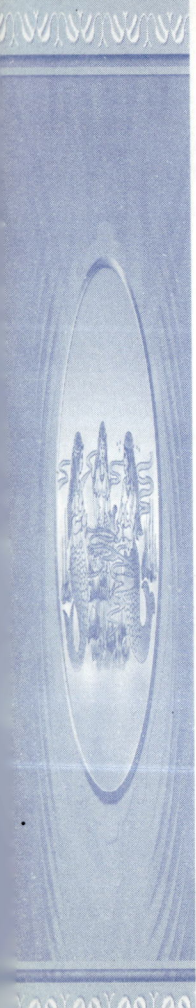

youth's raiment and swam silently and sorrowfully away. As they gathered together at a distance from the body of the dead soldier, one of them said, "The human heart is more severe than the cruel heart of Neptune."

WE AND YOU

WE are the sons of Sorrow, and you are the
Sons of Joy. We are the sons of Sorrow,
And Sorrow is the shadow of a God who
Lives not in the domain of evil hearts.

We are sorrowful spirits, and Sorrow is
Too great to exist in small hearts.
When you laugh, we cry and lament; and he
Who is seared and cleansed once with his
Own tears will remain pure forevermore.

You understand us not, but we offer our
Sympathy to you. You are racing with the

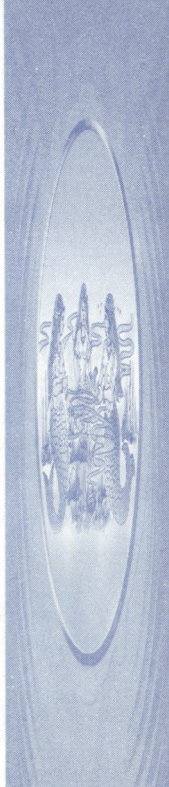

83

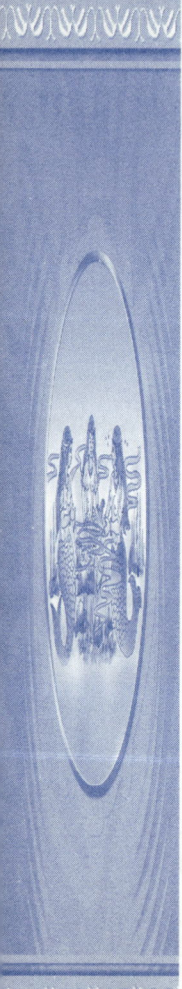

Current of the River of Life, and you
Do not look upon us; but we are sitting by
The coast, watching you and hearing your
Strange voices.

You do not comprehend our cry, for the
Clamour of the days is crowding your ears,
Blocked with the hard substance of your
Years of indifference to truth; but we hear
Your songs, for the whispering of the night

Has opened our inner hearts. We see you
Standing under the pointing finger of light,
But you cannot see us, for we are tarrying
In the enlightening darkness.

We are the sons of Sorrow; we are the poets
And the prophets and the musicians. We
weave
Raiment for the goddess from the threads of

Our hearts, and we fill the hands of the
Angels with the seeds of our inner selves.

You are the sons of the pursuit of earthly
Gaiety. You place your hearts in the hands
Of Emptiness, for the hand's touch to
Emptiness is smooth and inviting.

You reside in the house of Ignorance, for
In his house there is no mirror in which to
View your souls.

We sigh, and from our sighs arise the
Whispering of flowers and the rustling of
Leaves and the murmur of rivulets.

When you ridicule us your taunts mingle
With the crushing of the skulls and the
Rattling of shackles and the wailing of the
Abyss. When we cry, our tears fall into the

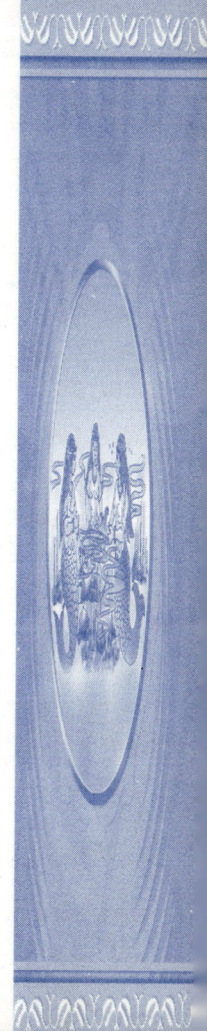

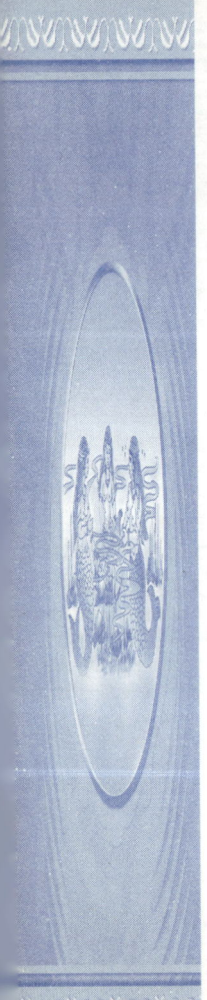

Heart of Life, As dew drops fall from the
Eyes of Night into the heart of Dawn; and
When you laugh, your mocking laughter
pours
Down like the viper's venom into a wound.

We cry, and sympathize with miserable
Wanderer and distressed widow; but you
rejoice
And smile at the sight of resplendent gold.

We cry, for we listen to the moaning of the
Poor and the grieving of the oppressed
weak,
But you laugh, for you hear naught but the
Happy sound of the wine goblets.

We cry, for our spirits are at the moment
Separated from God; but you laugh, for

your
Bodies cling with unconcern to the earth.
We are the sons of Sorrow, and you are the
Sons of Joy...Let us measure the outcome of
Our sorrow against the deeds of your joy
Before the face of the Sun....

You have built the Pyramids upon the hearts
Of slaves, but the Pyramids stand now upon
The sand, commemorating to the Ages our
Immortality and your evanescence.

You have built Babylon upon the bones of
the
Weak, and erected the palaces of Nineveh
upon
The graves of the miserable. Babylon is now
but

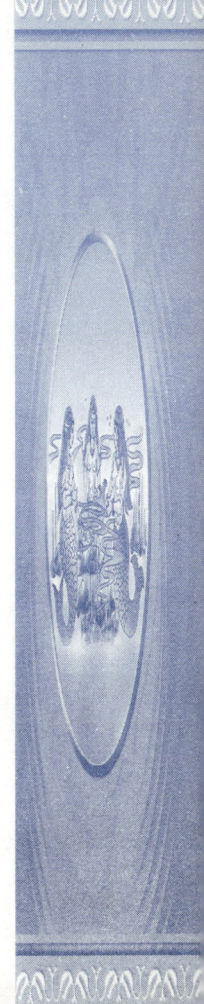

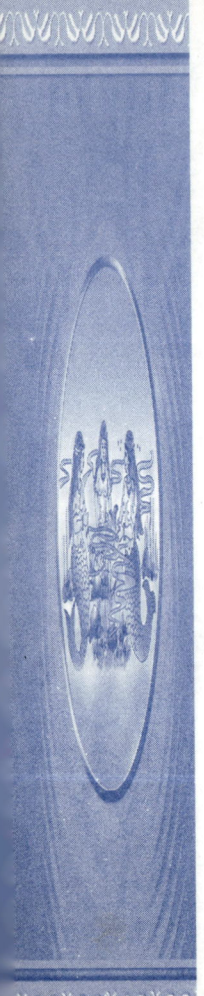

The footprint of the camel upon the moving
sand
Of the desert, and its history is repeated
To the nations who bless us and curse you.

We have carved Ishtar from solid marble,
And made it to quiver in its solidity and
Speak through its muteness.
We have composed and played the soothing
Song of Nahawand upon the strings, and
caused
The Beloved's spirit to come hovering in the
Firmament near to us; we have praised the
Supreme Being with words and deeds; the
words
Became as the words of God, and the deeds
Became overwhelming love of the angels.

You are following Amusement, whose
sharp claws
Have torn thousands of martyrs in the arenas
Of Rome and Antioch...But we are following
Silence, whose careful fingers have woven the
Iliad and the Book of Job and the
Lamentations Of Jeremiah.

You lie down with Lust, whose tempest has
Swept one thousand processions of the soul of
Woman away and into the pit of shame and
Horror...But we embrace Solitude, in whose
Shadow the beauties of Hamlet and Dante
arose.

You curry for the favor of Greed, and the
sharp
Swords of Greed have shed one thousand
rivers

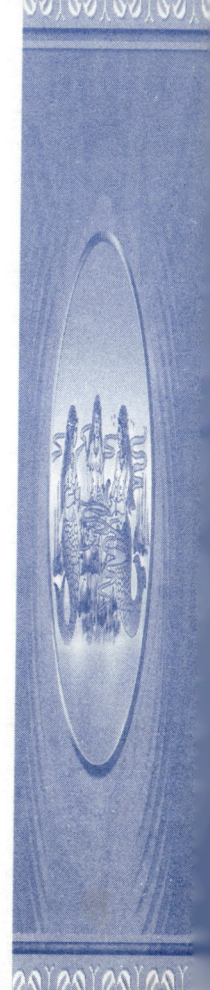

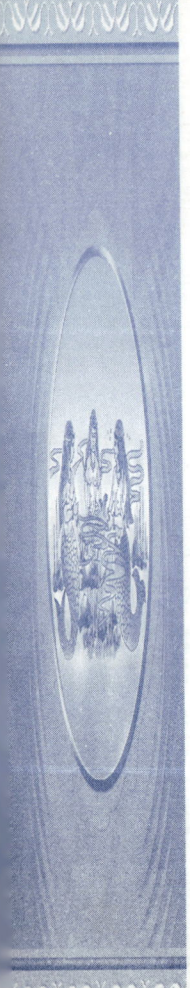

Of blood…But we seek company with Truth,
And the hands of Truth have brought
down
Knowledge from the Great Heart of the
Circle Of Light.
We are the sons of Sorrow, and you are the
Sons of Joy; and between our sorrow and
your
Joy there is a rough and narrow path which
Your spirited horses cannot travel, and upon
Which your magnificent carriages cannot
pass.

We pity your smallness as you hate our
Greatness; and between our pity and your
Hatred, Time halts bewildered. We come to
You as friends, but you attack us as
enemies;

And between our friendship and your
enmity,
There is a deep ravine flowing with tears
And blood.

We build palaces for you, and yoy dig
graves
For us; and between the beauty of the palace
And the obscurity of the grave, Humanity
Walks as a sentry with iron weapons.

We spread your path with roses, and you
cover
Our beds with thorns; and between the roses
And the thorns, Truth slumbers fitfully.

Since the beginning of the world you have
Fought against our gentle power with your
Coarse weakness; and when you triumph
over

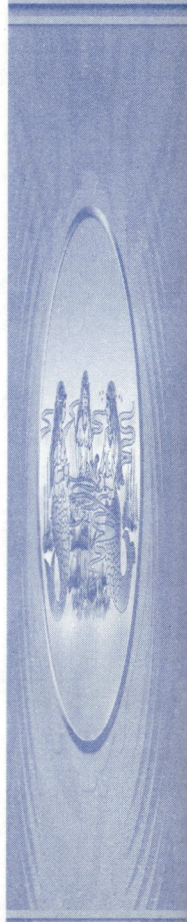

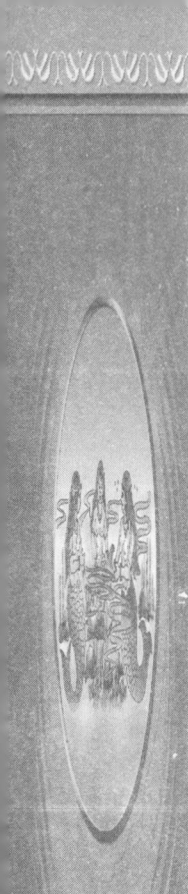

Us for an hour, you croak and clamour
merrily
Like the frogs of the water. And when we
Conquer you and subdue you for an Age,
we
Remain as silent giants.
You crucified Jesus and stood below Him,
Blaspheming and mocking at Him; but
at last
He came down and overcame the
generations,
And walked among you as a hero, filling
the
Universe with His glory and His beauty.

You poisoned Socrates and stoned Paul and
Destroyed Ali Talib and assassinated

Madhat Pasha, and yet those immortals are
With us forever before the face of Eternity.

But you live in the memory of man like
Corpses upon the face of the earth; and you
Cannot find a friend who will bury you in
The obscurity of non-existence and oblivion,
Which you sought on earth.
We are the sons of Sorrow, and sorrow is a
Rich cloud, showering the multitudes with
Knowledge and Truth. You are the sons of
Joy, and as high as your joy may reach,
By the Law of God it must be destroyed
Before the winds of heaven and dispersed
Into nothingness, for it is naught but a
Thin and wavering pillar of smoke.

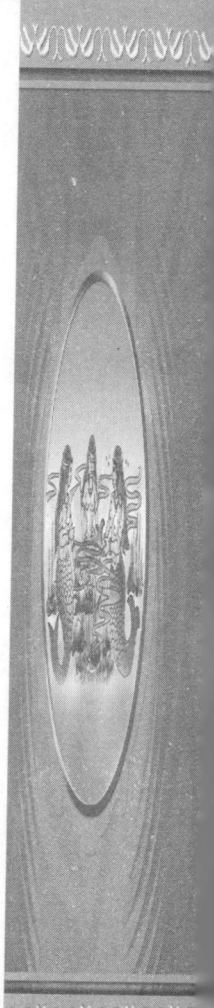

THE LONELY POET

I am a stranger in this world, and there is a severe solitude and painful lonesomeness in my exile. I am alone, but in my aloneness I contemplate an unknown and enchanting country, and this meditation fills my dreams with spectres of a great and distant land which my eyes have never seen.

I am a stranger among my people and I have no friends. When I see a person I say within myself, "Who is he, and in what manner do I know him, and why is he here, and what law has joined me with him?"

I am a stranger to myself, and when I hear

94

my tongue speak, my ears wonder over my voice; I see my inner self smiling, crying, braving, and fearing; and my existence wonders over my substance while my soul interrogates my heart; but I remain unknown, engulfed by tremendous silence.

My thoughts are strangers to my body, and as I stand before the mirror, I see something in my face which my soul does not see, and I find in my eyes what my inner self does not find.

When I walk vacant-eyed through the streets of the clamourous city, the children follow me, shouting, "Here is a blind man! Let us give him a walking cane to feel his way." When I run from them, I meet with a group of maidens, and they grasp the edges of my

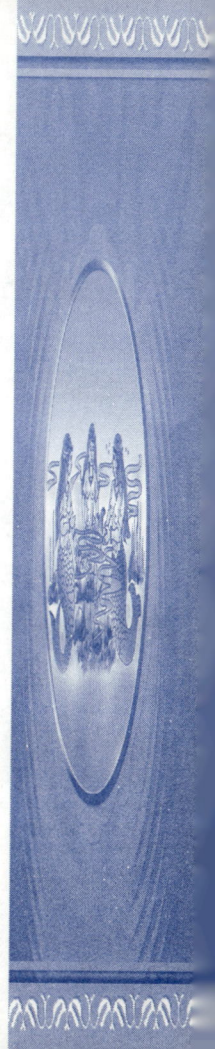

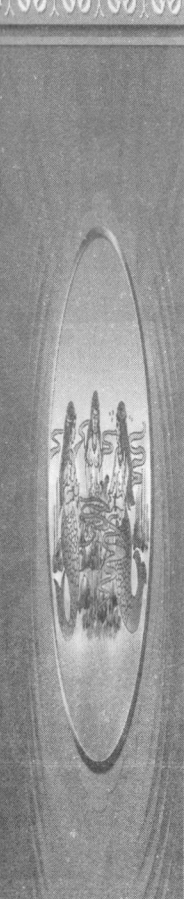

garment, saying, "He is deaf like the rock; let us fill his ears with the music of love." And when I flee from them, a throng of aged people point at me with trembling fingers and say, "He is a madman who lost his mind in the world of genii and ghouls."

I am a stranger in this world; I roamed the Universe from end to end, but could not find a place to rest my head; nor did I know any human I confronted, neither an individual who would hearken to my mind.

When I open my sleepless eyes at dawn, I find myself imprisoned in a dark cave from whose ceiling hang the insects and upon whose floor crawl the vipers.

When I go out to meet the light, the shadow of my body follows me, but the shadow of my spirit precedes me and leads the way to an unknown place seeking things beyond my understanding, and grasping objects that are meaningless to me.

At eventide I return and lie upon my bed, made of soft feathers and lined with thorns, and I contemplate and feel the troublesome and happy desires, and sense the painful and joyous hopes.

At midnight the ghosts of the past ages and the spirits of the forgotten civilization enter through the crevices of the cave to visit me......I stare at them and they gaze upon me; I talk to them and they answer me smilingly. Then I endeavour to clutch them, but they sift through my fingers and vanish like the mist which rests on the lake.

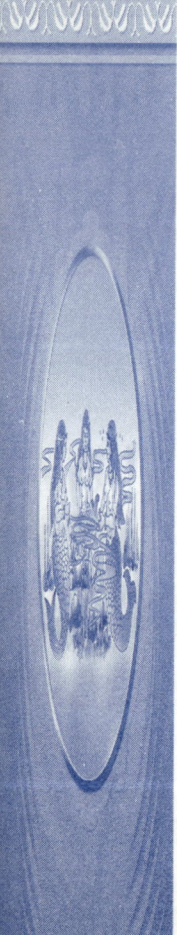

I am a stranger in this world, and there is no one in the Universe who understands the language I speak. Patterns of bizarre remembrance form suddenly in my mind, and my eyes bring forth queer images and sad ghosts. I walk in the deserted prairies, watching the streamlets running fast, up and up from the depths of the valley to the top of the mountain; I watch the naked trees blooming and bearing fruit, and shedding their leaves in one instant, and then I see the branches fall and turn into speckled snakes. I see the birds hovering above, singing and wailing; then they stop and open their wings and turn into undraped maidens with long hair, looking at me from behind kohled and infatuated eyes, and smiling at me with full lips soaked with honey, stretching their scented hands toward me. Then they ascend and disappear from my sight like phantoms, leaving in the firmament the resounding echo of their taunts and mocking laughter.

I am a stranger in this world….I am a poet who composes what life proses, and who proses what life composes.

For this reason I am a stranger, and I shall remain a stranger until the white and friendly wings of Death carry me home into my beautiful country, There, where light and peace and understanding abide, I will await the other strangers who will be rescued by the friendly trap of time from this narrow, dark world.

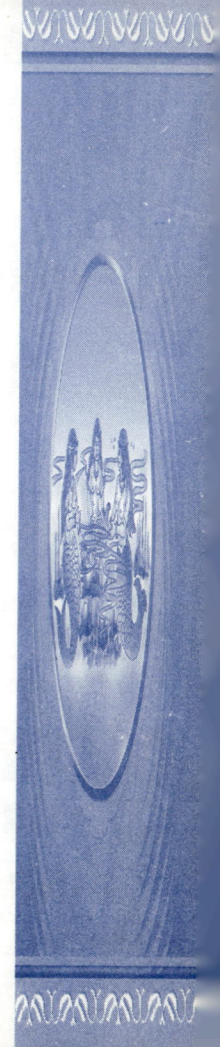

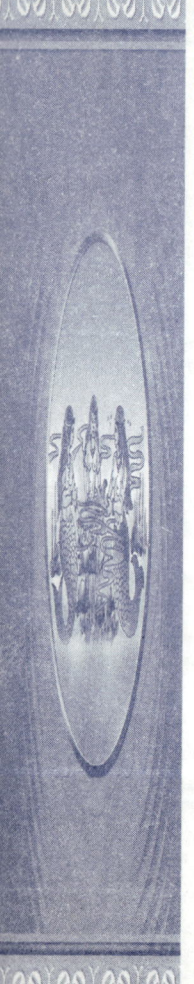

ASHES OF THE AGES AND ETERNAL FIRE

PART ONE

Spring of the Year 116 B.C

NIGHT had fallen and silence prevailed while life slumbered in the City of the Sun,* and the lamps were extinguished in the scattered houses about the majestic temples amidst the olive and laurel trees. The moon poured its silver rays upon the white marble

* Baalbek, or the City of Baal, called by the ancients "The City of the Sun," was built in honor of the Sun God Heliopolis, and historians assert that baalbek was the most beautiful city in the Middle East. Its ruins, which we observe at present time, indicate that the architecture was largly influenced by the Romans during the occupation of Syria (Editor's note.)

columns that stood like giants in the silence of the night, guarding the god's temples and looking with perplexity toward the towers of Lebanon that sat bristling upon the foreheads of the distant hills.

At that hour, while souls succumbed to the allure of slumber, Nathan, the son of the High Priest, entered Ishtar's temple, bearing a torch in trembling hands. He lighted the lamps and censers until the aromatic scent of myrrh and frankincense reached to the farthest corners; then he knelt before the altar, studded with inlays of ivory and gold, raised his hands toward Ishtar, and with a painful and choking voice he cried out, saying, "Have mercy upon me, O great Ishtar, goddess of Love and Beauty. Be merciful, and remove the hands of

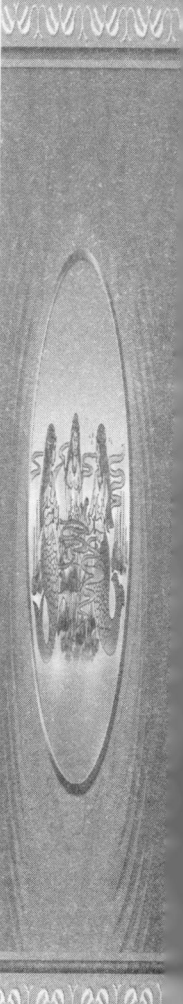

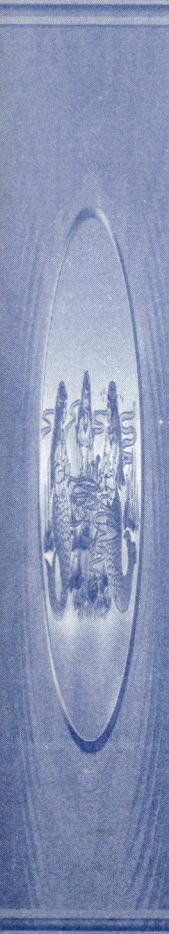

Death from my beloved, whom my soul has chosen by thy will.....The potions of the physicians and the wizards do not restore her life, neither the enchantments of the priests and the sorcerers. Naught is left to be done except thy holy will. Thou art my guide and my aid. Have mercy on me and grant my prayers! *Gaze upon my crushed heart and aching soul! Spare my beloved's life so that we may rejoice with the secrets of thy love, and glory in the beauty of youth that reveals the mystery of thy strength and wisdom. From the depths of my heart I cry unto thee, O exalted Ishtar, and

* *Ishtar was the great goddess of the Phoenicians. They worshipped her in the cities of Tyre, Sidon, Sur, Djabeil and Baalbek, and described her as the Burner of the Torch of Life, and Guardian of Youth. Greece adored her after Phoenicia, calling her the goddess of Love and Beauty. The Romans called her Venus.* (Editor's note.)

102

from behind the darkness of the night I beg thy mercy; hear me, O Ishtar! I am thy good servant Nathan, the son of the High Priest Hiram, and I devote all of my deeds and words to thy greatness at thy altar.

"I love a maiden amongst all maidens and made her my companion, but the genii brides envied her and blew into her body a strange affliction and sent unto her the messenger of Death who is standing by her bed like a hungry spectre, spreading his black ribbed wings over her, stretching forth his sharp claws in readiness to prey upon her. I come here now beseeching you to have mercy upon me and spare that flower who has not yet rejoiced with the summer of Life.

"Save her from the grasp of Death so we

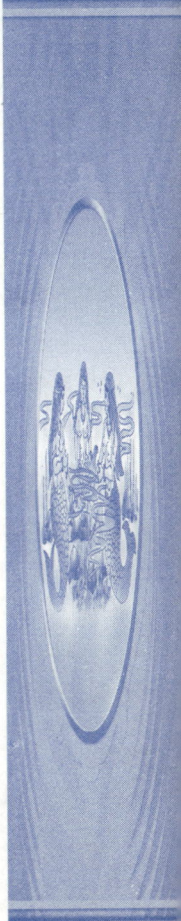

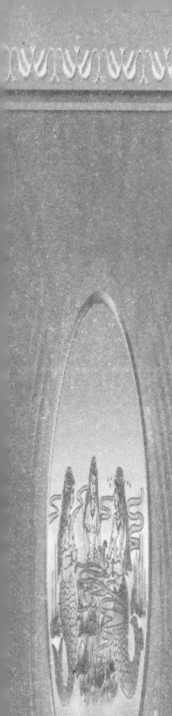

may sing joyfully thy praise and burn incense in thine honour and offer sacrifices at thy altar, filling thy vases with perfumed oil and spreading roses and violets upon the portico of thy place of worship, burning frankincense before thy shrine. Save her, O Ishtar, goddess of miracles and let Love overcome Death in this struggle of Joy against Sorrow."*

Nathan then became silent. His eyes were flooded with tears and his heart was uttering sorrowful sighs; then he continued, "Alas, my dreams are shattered, O Ishtar divine, and my heart is melted within; enliven me with thy mercy and spare my beloved."

*During the Era of Ignorance, the Arabs believed that if a genie loved a human youth, she would prevent him from marrying, and if he did wed, she would bewitch the bride and cause her to die. This mythological superstition persists today in some small villages in Lebanon. (Editor's note.)

At that moment one of his slaves entered the temple, hastened to Nathan, and whispered to him, "She has opened her eyes, Master, and looked about her bed, but could not find you; then she called for you, and I used all speed to advise you."

Nathan departed hurriedly and the slave followed him.

When he reached his palace, he entered the chamber of the ailing maiden, leaned over her bed, held her frail hand, and printed several kisses upon her lips as if striving to breathe into her body a new life from his own life. She moved her head on the silk cushions and opened her eyes. And upon her lips appeared the phantom of a smile which was the faint residue of life in her wasted body....the echo

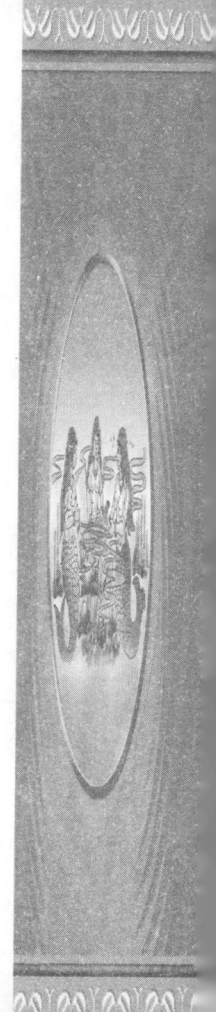

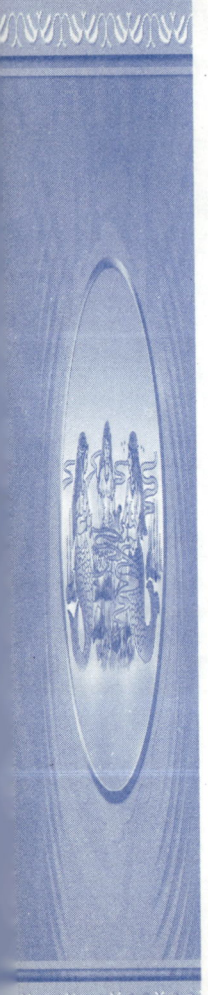

of the calling of a heart which is racing toward a halt; and with a voice that bespoke the weakening cries of a hungry infant on the breast of a withered mother, she said, "The goddess has called me, Oh Life of my Soul, and Death has come to sever me from you; but fear not, for the will of the goddess is sacred, and the demands of Death are just. I am departing now, and I hear the rustle of the whiteness descending, but the cups of Love and Youth are still full in our hands, and the flowered paths of beautiful Life are extended before us. I am embarking, My Beloved, upon an ark of the spirit, and I shall come back to this world, for great Ishtar will bring back to life those souls of loving humans who departed to Eternity before they enjoyed the sweetness of Love and the happiness of Youth.

"We shall meet again, Oh Nathan, and drink together the dew of the dawn from the cupped petals of the lilies, and rejoice with the birds of the fields over the colours of the rainbow. Until then, My Forever, farewell."*

Her voice lowered and her lips trembled like a lone flower before the gusts of dawn. Nathan embraced her with pouring tears, and as he pressed his lips upon her lips, he found them cold as the stone of the field. He uttered a terrible cry and commenced tearing his raiment;

* *Many Asiatics pursue this belief with conviction, having derived it from their holy writings. Mohammed said, "You were dead and He brought you back to life, and He will deaden you again and then will enliven you, whereupon you shall go back to Him." Buddha said, "Yesterday we existed in this life, and now we came, and we will continue to go back until we become perfect like the God."* (Editor's note.)

107

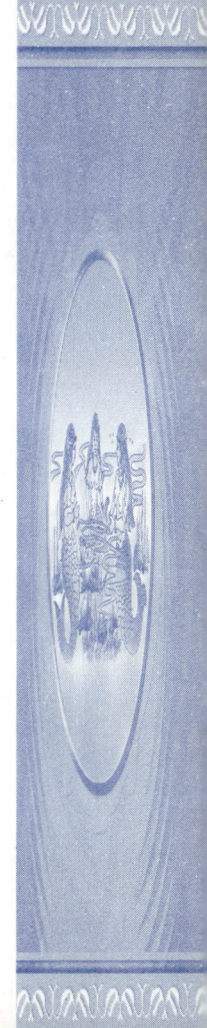

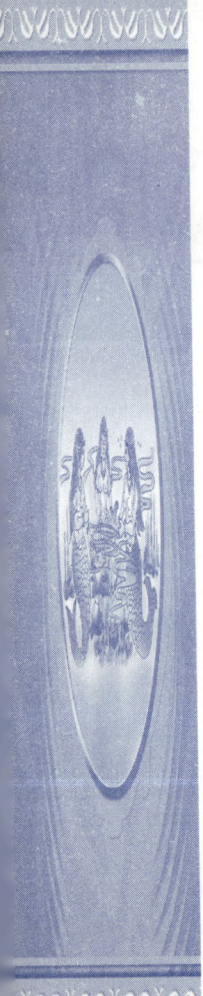

he threw himself upon her dead body while his shivering soul was sailing fitfully between the mountain of Life and the precipice of Death.

In the silence of the night, the slumbering souls were awakened. Women and children were frightened as they heard mighty rumbling and painful wailing and bitter lamentation coming from the corners of the palace of the High Priest of Ishtar.

When the tired morn arrived, the people asked about Nathan to offer their sympathy, but were told that he had disappeared. And after a fortnight, the chief of a caravan arriving from the East related that he had seen Nathan in the distant wilderness, wandering with a flock of gazelles.

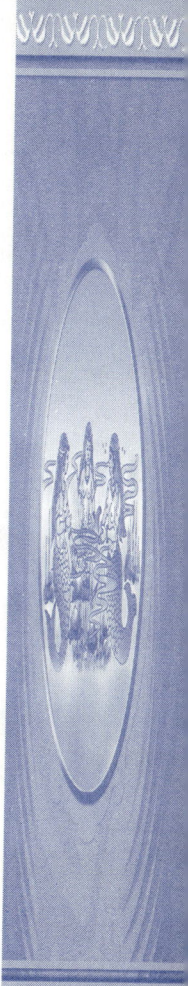

The ages passed, crushing with their invisible feet the feeble acts of the civilizations, and the goddess of Love and Beauty had left the country. A strange and fickle goddess took her place. She destroyed the magnificent temples of the City of the Sun and demolished its beautiful palaces. The blooming orchards and fertile prairies were laid waste and nothing was left in that spot save ruins commemorating to the aching souls the ghosts of Yesterday, repeating to the sorrowful spirits only the echo of the hymns of glory.

But the severe ages that crushed the deeds of man could not destroy his dreams; nor could they weaken his love, for dreams and affections are ever-living with the Eternal Spirit. They may disappear for a time, pursuing the

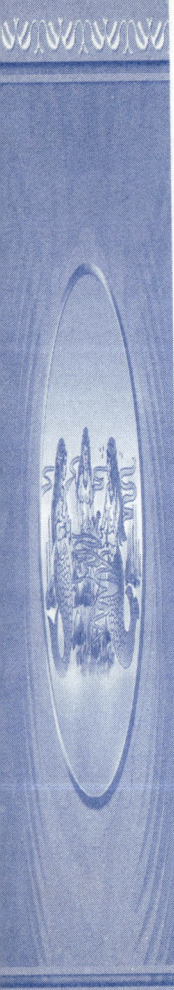

sun when the night comes, and the stars when morning appears, but like the lights of heaven, they must surely return.

PART TWO

Spring of the Year 1890 A.D.

The day was over, Nature was making her many preparations for slumber, and the sun withdrew its golden rays from the plains of Baalbek. Ali El Hosseini* brought his herd back to the shed in the midst of the ruins of the temples. He sat there near the ancient columns which symbolized the bones of countless soldiers left behind in the field of

---

*The Hosseinese are groups comprising an Arabian tribe, at present living in tents pitched in the plains surrounding the ruins of Baalbek. (Editor's note.)

110

battle. The sheep folded around him, charmed with the music of his flute.

Midnight came, and heaven sowed the seeds of the following day in the deep furrows of the darkness. Ali's eyes became tired of the phantoms of awakeness, and his mind was wearied by the procession of ghosts marching in horrible silence amidst the demolished walls. He leaned upon his arm, and sleep captured his senses with the extreme end of its plaited veil, like a delicate cloud touching the face of a calm lake. He forgot his actual self and encountered his invisible self, rich with dreams and ideals higher than the laws and teachings of man. The circle of vision broadened before his eyes, and Life's hidden secrets gradually became apparent to him. His soul abandoned

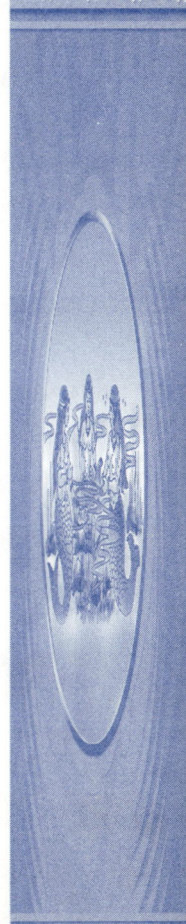

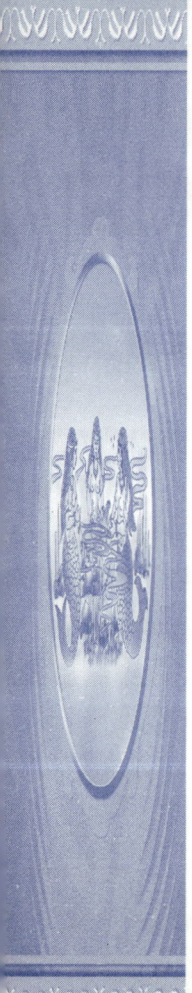

the rapid parade of time rushing toward nothingness; it stood alone before symmetrical thoughts and crystal ideas. For the first time in his life, Ali was aware of the causes for the spiritual famine that had accompanied his youth....The famine which levels away the pit between the sweetness and the bitterness of Life....That thirst which unites into contentment the sighs of Affection and the silence of Satisfaction....That longing which cannot be vanquished by the glory of the world nor twisted by the passing of the ages. Ali felt the surge of a strange affection and a kind tenderness within himself which was Memory, enlivening itself like incense placed upon white firebrands.....It was a magic love whose soft fingers had touched Ali's heart as a musician's delicate fingers touch quivering strings. It was a new power emanating from nothingness and growing forcefully, embracing his real self and filling his spirit with ardent love, at once painful and sweet.

Ali looked toward the ruins and his heavy eyes became alert as he fancied the glory of those devastated shrines that stood as mighty, impregnable, and eternal temples long before. His eyes became motionless and the breathing of his heart quickened. And like a blind man whose sight has suddenly been restored, he commenced to see, think and meditate….He recollected the lamps and the silver censers that surrounded the image of an adored and revered goddess…He remembered the priests offering sacrifices before an altar built of ivory and

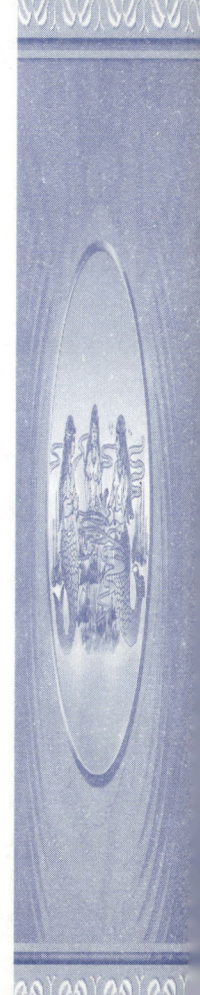

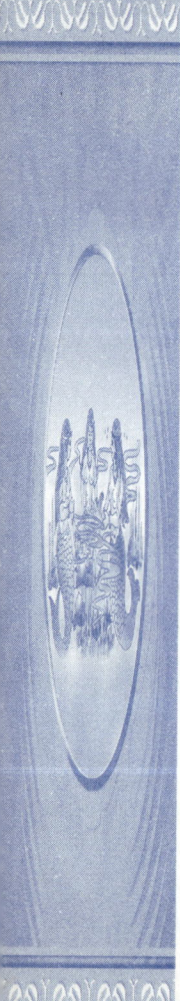

gold....He envisioned the dancing maidens, and the tambourine players, and the singers who chanted the praise of the goddess of Love and Beauty; he saw all this before him, and felt the impression of their obscurity in the choking depths of his heart.

But memory alone brings naught save echoes of voices heard in the depths of the long ago. What, then, is the bizarre relationship between these powerful, weaving memories and the past actual life of a simple youth who was born in a tent and who spent the spring of his life grazing sheep in the valleys?

Ali gathered himself and walked amidst the ruins, and the gnawing memories suddenly tore the veil of oblivion from his thoughts. As he reached the great and cavernous entrance to the temple, he halted as if a magnetic power gripped him and fastened his feet. As he looked downward, he found a smashed status on the ground. He broke from the grasp of the Unseen and at once his soul's tears unleashed and poured like blood issuing from a deep wound; his heart roared in ebb and flow like the welling waves of the sea. He sighed bitterly and cried painfully, for he felt a stabbing aloneness and a destructive remoteness standing as an abyss between his heart and the heart from whom he was torn before he entered upon this life. He felt that his soul's element was but a flame from the burning torch which God had separated from Himself before the passing of the Ages. He perceived the feathery touch of delicate wings rustling about his flaming heart, and a great love possessing

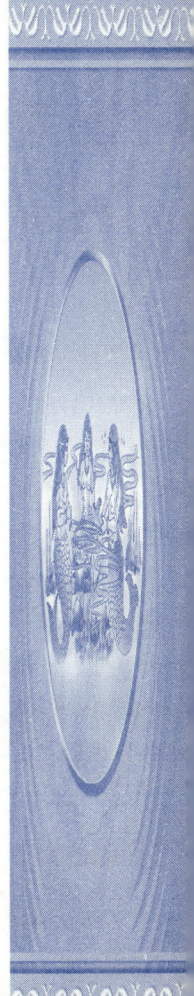

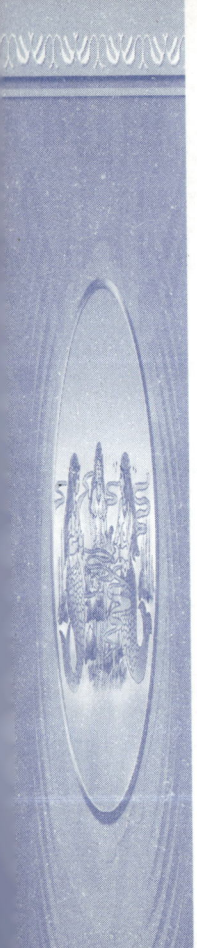

him....A love whose power separates the mind from the world of quantity and measurement....A love that talks when the tongue of Life is muted....A love that stands as a blue beacon to point out the path, guiding with no visible light. That love or that God who descended in that quiet hour upon Ali's heart had seared into his being a bitter and sweet affection, like thorns growing by the side of the flourishing flowers.

But who is this Love and whence did he come? What does he desire of a shepherd kneeling in the midst of those ruins? Is it a seed sown without awareness in the domain of the heart by a Bedouin maiden? Or a beam appeared from behind the dark cloud to illuminate life? Is it a dream that crept close in the silence of the night to ridicule him? Or is it Truth that existed since the Beginning, and shall continue to exist until the Ending?

Ali closed his tearful eyes and stretched forth his arms like a beggar, and exclaimed, "Who are you, standing close to my heart but away from my sight, yet acting as a great wall between me and my real self, binding my today with my forgotten past? Are you the phantom of a spectre from Eternity to show me the vanity of Life and the weakness of mankind? Or the spirit of a genie appeared from the earth's crevices to enslave me and render me an object of mockery amongst the youths of my tribe? Who are you and what is this strange power which at one time deadens and enlivens my heart? Who am I and what is this strange

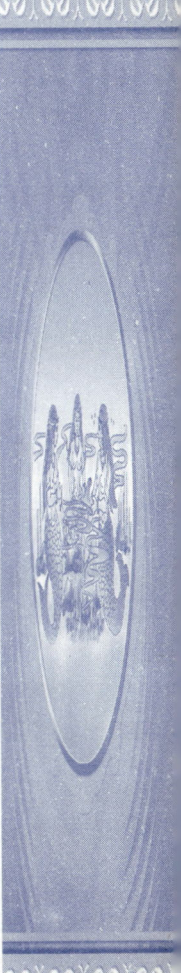

self whom I call "Myself?" Has the Water of Life which I drank made of me an angel, seeing and hearing the mysterious secrets of the Universe, or is it merely an evil wine that intoxicated me and blinded me from myself?"

He became silent, while his anxiety grew and his spirit exulted. Then he continued, "Oh, that which the soul reveals, and the night conceals....Oh, beautiful spirit, hovering in the sky of my dream; you have awakened in me a dormant fullness, like healthy seeds hidden under the blankets of snow; you have passed me like a frolicsome breeze carrying to my hungry self the fragrance of the flowers of heaven; you have touched my senses and agitated and quivered them like the leaves of the trees. Let me look upon you now if you are a human, or command Slumber to shut my eyes so I can view your vastness through my inner being. Let me touch you; let me hear your voice. Tear away this veil that conceals my entire purpose, and destroy this wall that hides my deity from my clearing eyes, and place upon me a pair of wings so I may fly behind you to the halls of the Supreme Universe. Or bewitch my eyes so I may follow you to the ambush of the genii if you are one of their brides. If I am worthy, place your hand upon my heart and possess me."

Ali was whispering these words into the mystic darkness, and before him crept the ghosts of night, as if they were vapour coming from his boiling tears. Upon the walls of the temple he fancied magical pictures painted with the brush of the rainbow.

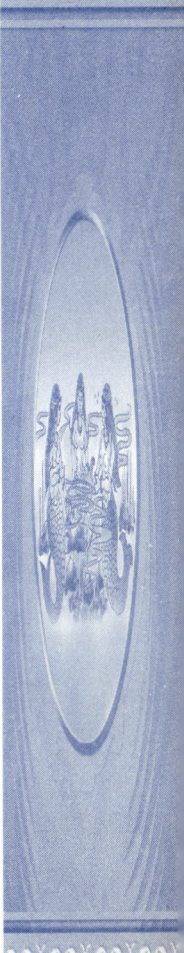

119

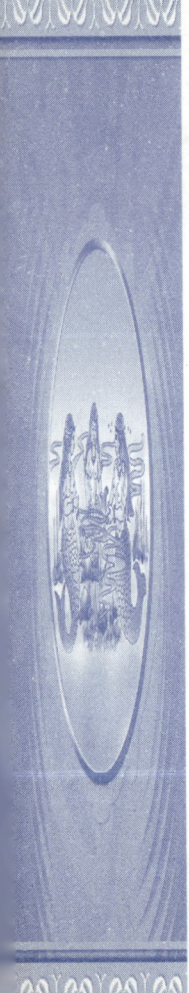

Thus did one hour pass, with Ali shedding tears and reveling in his miserable plight and hearing the beats of his heart, looking beyond the objects as if he were observing the images of Life vanishing slowly and being replaced with a dream, strange in its beauty and terrible in enormity. Like a prophet who meditates the stars of heaven awaiting the Descent and Revelation, he pondered the power existing beyond these contemplations. He felt that his spirit left him and probed through the temples for a priceless but unknown segment of himself, lost among the ruins.

Dawn had appeared and silence roared with the passing of the breeze; the first rays of light raced through, illuminating the particles of the ether, and the sky smiled like a dreamer viewing his beloved's phantom. The birds probed from their sanctuary in the crevices of the walls and emerged into the halls of the columns, singing their morning prayers.

Ali placed his cupped hand over his forehead, looking downward with glazed eyes. Like Adam, when God opened his eyes with Almighty breath, Ali saw new objects, strange and fantastic. Then he approached his sheep and called to them, whereupon they followed him quietly toward the lush fields. He led them, as he gazed at the sky like a philosopher divining and meditating the secrets of the Universe. He reached a brook whose murmuring was soothing to the spirit, and he sat by the edge of the spring under the willow tree, whose branches dipped over the water as

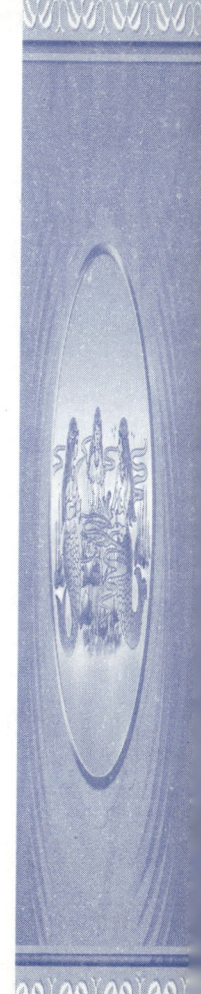

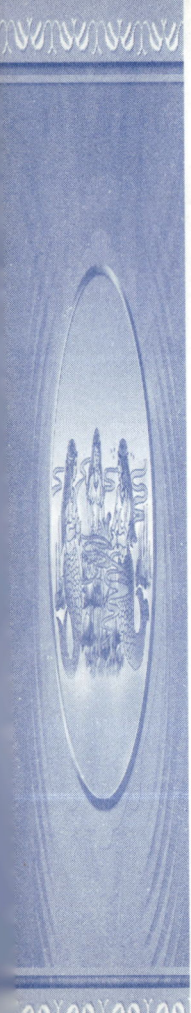

if drinking from the cool depths. The dew of dawn glistened upon the sheep's wool as they grazed amid flowers and green grass.

In a few moments Ali again felt that his heartbeats were increasing rapidly and his spirit commenced to vibrate violently, almost visibly. Like a mother suddenly awakened from her slumber by the scream of her child, he bolted from his position, and as his eyes were compelled to her, he saw a beautiful maiden carrying an earthenware container upon her shoulder, slowly approaching the far side of the brook. As she reached the edge and leaned forward to fill the jar, she glanced across, and her eyes met Ali's eyes. As if in insanity she cried out, dropped the jar, and withdrew swiftly. Then she turned, gazing at Ali with anxious, agonizing disbelief.

A minute passed, whose seconds were glittering lamps illuminating their hearts and spirits, and silence brought vague remembrance, revealing to them images and scenes far away from that brook and those trees. They heard each other in the understanding silence, listening tearfully to each other's sighs of heart and soul until complete knowing prevailed between the two.

Ali, still compelled by a mysterious power, leaped across the brook and approached the maiden, embraced her and printed a long kiss upon her lips, As if the sweetness of Ali's caress had usurped her will, she did not move, and the kind touch of Ali's arms had stolen her strength. She yielded to him as the fragrance of jasmine concedes to the vibration of the breeze, carrying it into the spacious firmament.

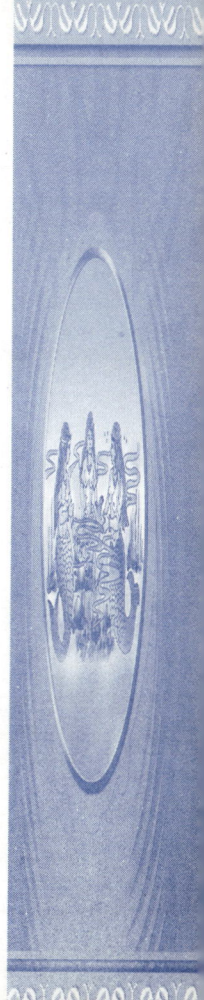

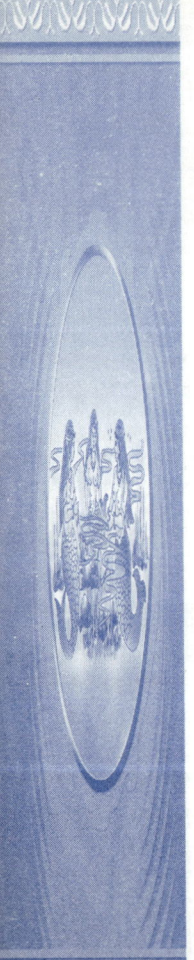

She placed her head upon his chest like a tortured person who has found rest. She sighed deeply....a sigh that announced the rebirth of happiness in a torn heart and proclaimed a revolution of wings that had ascended after having been injured and committed to earth.

She raised her head and looked at him with her soul.....the look of a human which, in mighty silence, belittles the conventional words used amongst mankind; the expression which offers myriads of thoughts in the unspoken language of the hearts. She bore the look of a person who accepts Love not as a spirit in a body of words, but as a reunion occurring long after two souls were divided by earth and joined by God.

The enamoured couple walked amidst the

willow trees, and the singleness of two selves was a speaking tongue for their unification; a seeing eye for the glory of Happiness; a silent listener to the tremendous revelation of Love.

The sheep continued grazing, and the birds of the sky still hovered above their heads, singing the song of Dawn, following the emptiness of night. As they reached the end of the valley the sun appeared, spreading a golden garment upon the knolls and the hills, and they sat by the side of a rock where the violets hid. The maiden looked into Ali's black eyes while the breeze caressed her hair, as if the shimmering wisps were fingertips craving for sweet kisses. She felt as though some magic and strong gentleness were touching her lips in spite of her will, and with a serene and

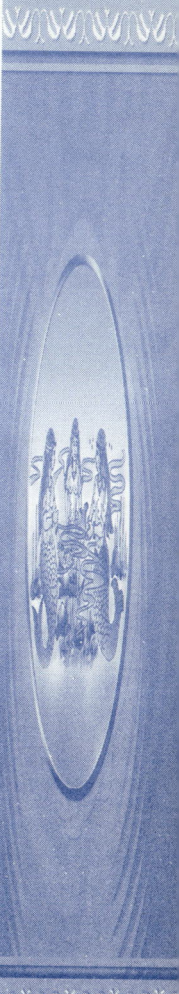

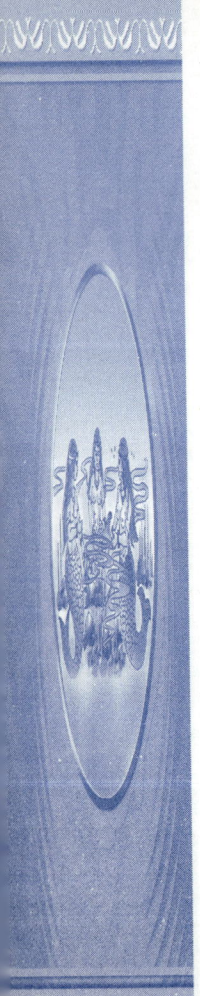

charming voice she said, "Ishtar has restored both of our spirits to this life from another, so we may not be denied the joy of Love and the glory of Youth, my beloved."

Ali closed his eyes, as if her musical voice brought to him images of a dream he had seen, and he felt an invisible pair of wings carrying him from that place and depositing him in a strange chamber by the side of a bed upon which lay the corpse of a maiden whose beauty had been claimed by Death. He cried fearfully, then opened his eyes and found that same maiden sitting by his side, and upon her lips appeared a smile. Her eyes shone with the rays of Life. Ali's face brightened and his heart was refreshed. The phantom of his vision withdrew slowly until he forgot completely the past and its cares. The two lovers embraced and drank the wine of sweet kisses together until they became intoxicated. They slumbered, wrapped between each other's arms, until the last remnant of the shadow was dispersed by the Eternal Power which had awakened them.

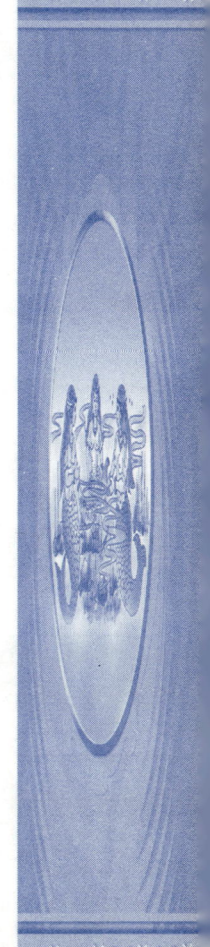

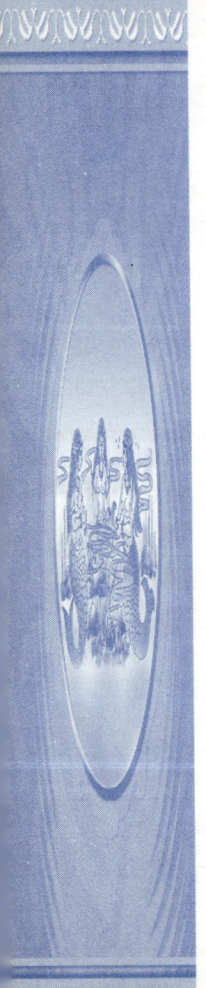

BETWEEN NIGHT AND MORN

B E SILENT, my heart, for the space cannot
Hear you; be silent, for the ether is
Laden with cries and moans, and cannot
Carry your songs and hymns.

Be silent, for the phantoms of the night
Will not give heed to the whispering of
Your secrets; nor will the processions
Of darkness halt before your dreams.

Be silent, my heart, until Dawn comes,
For he who patiently awaits the morn
Will meet him surely, and he who loves

The light will be loved by the light.

Be silent, my heart, and hearken to my
Story; in my dream I saw a nightingale
Singing over the throat of a fiery
Volcano, and I saw a lily raising her
Head above the snow, and a naked Houri
Dancing in the midst of the graves, and
An infant playing with skulls while
Laughing.

I saw all these images in my dream, and
When I opened my eyes and looked about
Me, I saw the volcano still raging, but
No longer heard the nightingale sing;
Nor did I see him hovering.

I saw the sky spreading snow upon the
Fields and valleys, and concealing under

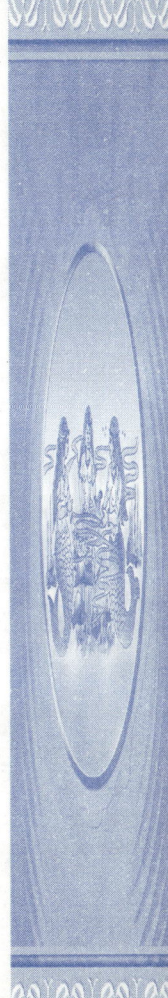

White shrouds the stilled bodies of the
Lilies. I saw a row of graves before
The silence of the Ages, but there was
No person dancing or praying in their
Midst. I saw a heap of skulls, but no
One was there to laugh, save the wind.

In my awakeness I saw grief and sorrow;
What became of the joy and sweetness of
My dream? Where has the beauty of my
Dream gone, and in what manner did the
Images disappear?

How can the soul be patient until Slumber
Restores the happy phantoms of hope and
Desire?

Give heed, my heart, and hear my story;
Yesterday my soul was like an old and

Strong tree, whose roots grasped into the
Depths of the earth, and whose branches
Reached the Infinite. My soul blossomed
In Spring, and gave fruit in Summer, and
When Autumn came, I gathered the fruit on
A silver tray and placed it by the
Walkers's portion of the street; and all
Who passed partook willingly and continued
To walk.

And when Autumn passed away, and
submerged
His rejoicing under wailing and lamentation,
I looked upon my tray and found but one
Fruit remaining; I took it and placed it
Into my mouth, but found it bitter as gall,
And sour as the hard grapes, and I said to
Myself, "Woe to me, for I have placed a

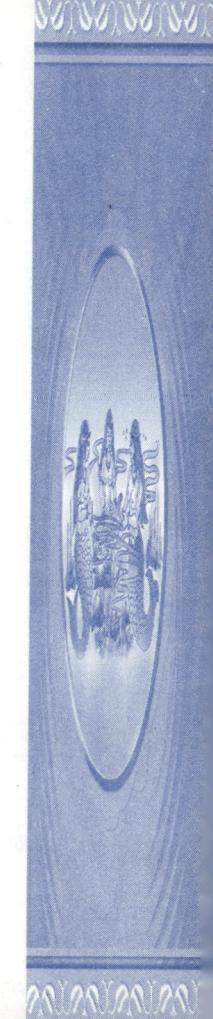

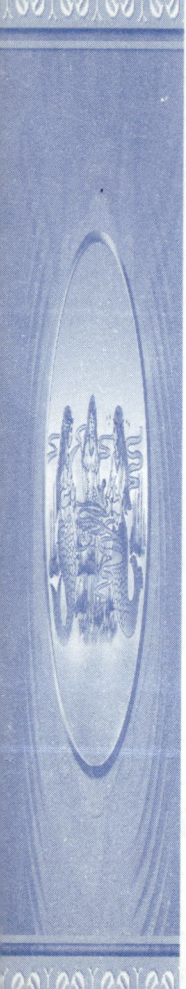

Curse in the mouths of the people, and an
Ailment in their bodies. What have you
Done, my soul, with the sweet sap which
Your roots have sucked from the earth, and
The fragrance which you have drawn from
The sky?" In anger did I tear the strong
And old tree of my soul, with each of the
Struggling roots, from the depths of the
Earth.

I uprooted it from the past, and took
From it the memories of one thousand
Springs and one thousand Autumns, and I
Planted the tree of my soul in another
Place. It was now in a field afar from
The path of Time; and I tended it in day
And in night, saying within me,
"Wakefulness

Will bring us closer to the stars.

I watered it with blood and tears, saying,
"There is a flavour in blood, and a
Sweetness in tears." When Spring returned,
My tree bloomed again, and in the Summer it
Bore fruit. And when Autumn came, I
gathered
All the ripe fruit upon a golden plate and
Offered it in the public path, and the people
Passed but none desired my fruit.

Then I took one fruit and brought it to my
Lips, and it was sweet as the honeycomb
And exhilarating as the wine of Babylon
And fragrant as the jasmine. And I cried
Out, saying, "The people do not want a
Blessing in their mouths, nor a truth in

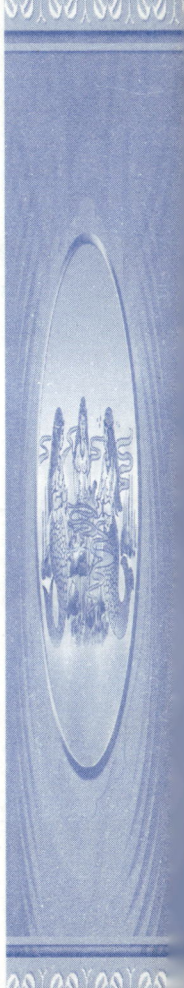

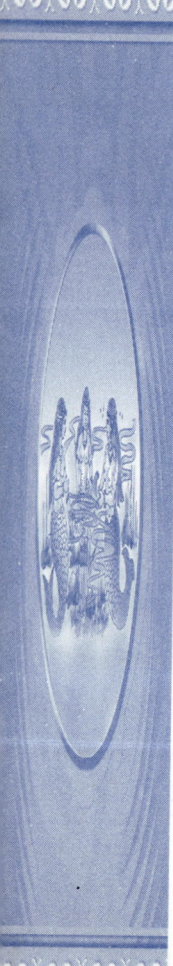

Their hearts, for Blessing is the daughter
Of Tears, and Truth is the son of Blood."

I left the noisome city to sit in the shadow
Of the solitary tree of my soul, in a
Field far from life's path.

Be silent, my heart, until Dawn comes;
Be silent and attend my story;
Yesterday my thoughts were a boat sailing
Amidst the waves in the sea, and moving
With the winds from one land to another.
And my boat was empty except of seven
Jars of rainbow colours; and the time
Came when I grew weary of moving about
On the face of the sea, and I said to
Myself, "I shall return with the empty
Boat of my thoughts to the harbour of the
Isle of my birth."

And I prepared by colouring my boat yellow
Like the sunset, and green like the heart
Of spring, and blue like the sky, and red
Like the anemone. And on the masts and
On the rudder I drew strange figures that
Compelled the attention and dazzled the
Eye. And as I ended my task, the boat of
My thoughts seemed as a prophetic vision,
Sailing between the two infinities, the
Sea and the sky.

I entered the harbour of the isle of my
Birth, and the people surged to meet me
With singing and merriment. And the
Throngs invited me to enter the city;
And they were plucking their instruments
And sounding their tambourines.

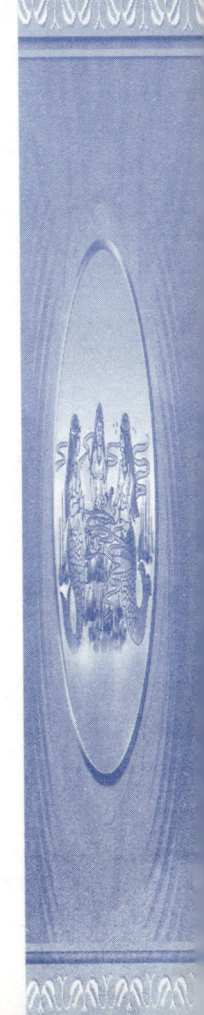

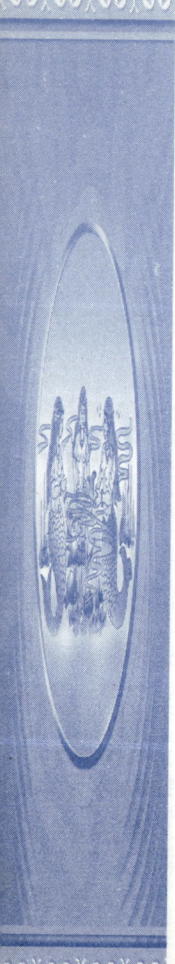

Such welcome was mine because my boat
Was beautifully decorated, and none
Entered and saw the interior of the
Boat of my thoughts, nor asked what
I had brought from beyond the seas. Nor
Could they observe that I had brought
My boat back empty, for its brilliance
Had rendered them blind. Thereupon I
Said within myself, "I have led the
People astray, and with seven jars of
Colours I have cheated their eyes."

Thereafter, I embarked in the boat of
My thoughts, again to set sail. I
Visited the East Islands and gathered
Myrrh, frankincense and sandalwood, and
Placed them in my boat.....I roamed the
West Islands and brought ivory and ruby

And emerald and many rare gems...I
Journeyed the South Islands and carried
Back with me beautiful armours and
Glittering swords and spears and all
Varieties of weapons....I filled the
Boat of my thoughts with the choicest
And most precious things on earth, and
Returned to the harbour of the isle of
My birth, saying, "The people shall again
Glorify me, but with honesty, and they
Shall again invite me to enter their
City, but with merit."

And when I reached the harbour, none
Came to meet me.....I walked the streets
Of my earlier glory but no person looked
Upon me....I stood in the market place
Shouting to the people of the treasures

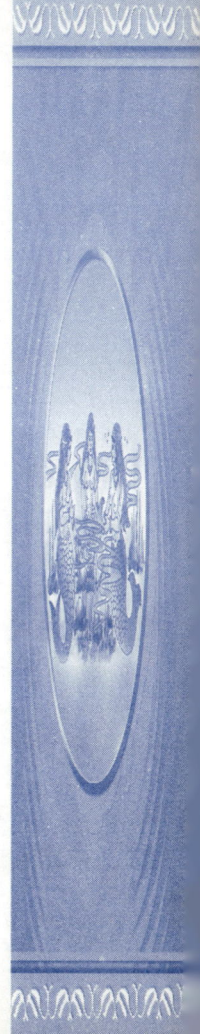

In my boat, and they mocked at me and
Heeded not.

I returned to the harbour with spiritless
Heart and disappointment and confusion.
And when I gazed upon my boat, I observed
A thing which I had not seen during my
Voyage, and I exclaimed, "The waves of
The sea have done away with the colours
and
The figures on my boat and caused it to
look
Like a skeleton." The winds and the spray
Together with the burning sun had effaced
The brilliant hues and my boat looked now
Like tattered grey raiment. I could not
Observe these changes from amid my
treasures,

For I had blinded my eyes from the inside.

I had gathered the most precious things on
Earth and placed them in a floating chest
Upon the face of the water and returned to
My people, but they cast me away and
could
Not see me, for their eyes had been allured
By empty, shimmering objects.

At that hour I left the boat of my thoughts
For the City of the Dead, and sat in the
Midst of the trim graves, contemplating
Their secrets.

Be silent, my heart, until Dawn comes; be
Silent, for the raging tempest is ridiculing
Your inner whispering, and the caves of
The valleys do not echo the vibration of

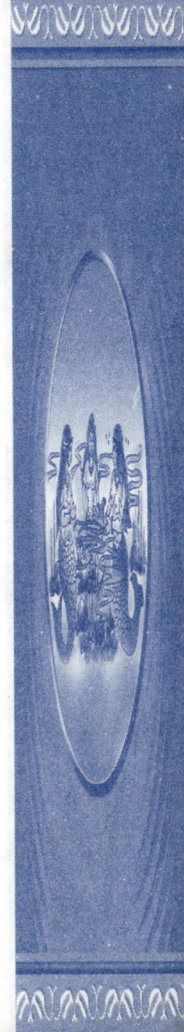

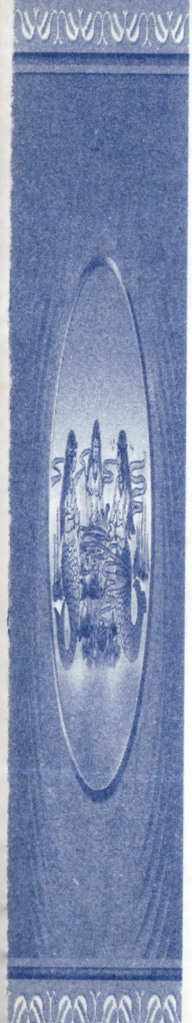

Your strings.

Be silent, my heart, until Morn comes
For he who awaits patiently the coming
Of Dawn will be embraced longingly by
Morningtide.

Dawn is breaking. Speak if you are able,
My heart. Here is the procession of
Morningtide....Why do you not speak?
Has not the silence of the night left
A song in your inner depths with which
You may meet Dawn?
Here are the swarms of doves and the
Nightingales moving in the far portion
Of the valley. Are you capable of flying
With the birds, or has the horrible night
Weakened your wings? The shepherds are

Leading the sheep from their folds; has
The phantom of the night left strength
In you so you may walk behind them to
The green prairies? The young men and
Women are walking gracefully toward the
Vineyards. Will you be able to stand
And walk with them? Rise, my heart and
Walk with Dawn, for the night has passed,
And the fear of darkness has vanished with
Its black dreams and ghastly thoughts and
Insane travels.

Rise, my heart, and raise your voice with
Music, for he who shares not Dawn with
His songs is one of the sons of ever-
Darkness.

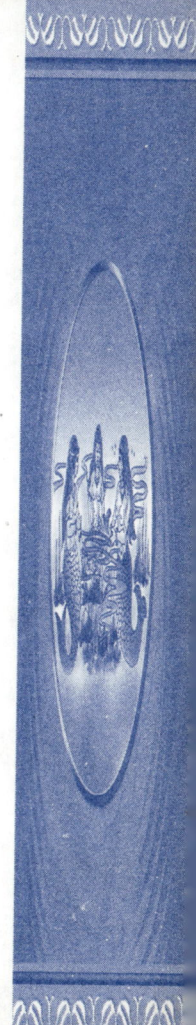